The Anti-Aesthetic
ESSAYS ON POSTMODERN CULTURE

The Anti-Aesthetic

ESSAYS ON POSTMODERN CULTURE

Edited by Hal Foster

BAY PRESS   **1983**

Port Townsend, Washington

Copyright © 1983 by Bay Press
All rights reserved
Printed in the United States of America
First edition published in 1983
Second printing 1984
Bay Press
3710 Discovery Road North
Port Townsend, WA 98368

Library of Congress Cataloging in Publication Data
Main entry under title:

The Anti-aesthetic.

1. Modernism (Aesthetics) — Addresses, essays, lectures.
2. Civilization, Modern — 1950 — Addresses, essays, lectures.
I. Foster, Hal.
BH301.M54A57   1983   909.82   83-70650
ISBN 0-941920-02-X
ISBN 0-941920-01-1 (pbk.)

Contributors

JEAN BAUDRILLARD, Professor of Sociology at the University of Paris, is the author of *The Mirror of Production* (Telos, 1975) and *For a Critique of the Political Economy of the Sign* (Telos, 1981).

DOUGLAS CRIMP is a critic and Managing Editor of *October*.

HAL FOSTER (Editor) is a critic and Associate Editor at *Art in America*.

KENNETH FRAMPTON, Professor at the Graduate School of Architecture and Planning, Columbia University, is the author of *Modern Architecture* (Oxford University Press, 1980).

JÜRGEN HABERMAS, presently associated with the Max Planck Institute in Starnberg, Germany, is the author of *Knowledge and Human Interests* (Beacon Press, 1971), *Theory and Practice* (Beacon Press, 1973), *Legitimation Crisis* (Beacon Press, 1975) and *Communication and the Evolution of Society* (Beacon Press, 1979).

FREDRIC JAMESON, Professor of Literature and History of Consciousness, University of California at Santa Cruz, is the author of *Marxism and Form* (Princeton University Press, 1971), *The Prison-House of Language* (Princeton University Press, 1972), *Fables of Aggression* (University of California Press, 1979) and *The Political Unconscious* (Cornell University Press, 1981).

ROSALIND KRAUSS, Professor of Art History at the City University of New York, is the author of *Terminal Iron Works: The Sculpture of David Smith* (MIT Press, 1972) and *Passages in Modern Sculpture* (Viking Press, 1977). She is Co-Editor of *October*.

CRAIG OWENS is a critic and Senior Editor at *Art in America*.

EDWARD W. SAID, Parr Professor of English and Comparative Literature at Columbia University, is the author of *Beginnings* (Basic Books, 1975), *Orientalism* (Pantheon Books, 1978), *Covering Islam* (Pantheon Books, 1981) and *The World, The Text and the Critic* (Harvard University Press, 1983).

GREGORY L. ULMER, Associate Professor of English, at the University of Florida, Gainesville, has recently completed a book-length study, "Applied Grammatology: Post(e)-Pedagogy from Jacques Derrida to Joseph Beuys."

Contents

Postmodernism: A Preface

HAL FOSTER

Postmodernism: does it exist at all and, if so, what does it mean? Is it a concept or a practice, a matter of local style or a whole new period or economic phase? What are its forms, effects, place? How are we to mark its advent? Are we truly beyond the modern, truly in (say) a postindustrial age?

The essays in this book take up these questions and many others besides. Some critics, like Rosalind Krauss and Douglas Crimp, define postmodernism as a break with the aesthetic field of modernism. Others, like Gregory Ulmer and Edward Said, engage the "object of post-criticism" and the politics of interpretation today. Some, like Fredric Jameson and Jean Baudrillard, detail the postmodern moment as a new, "schizophrenic" mode of space and time. Others, like Craig Owens and Kenneth Frampton, frame its rise in the fall of modern myths of progress and mastery. But all the critics, save Jürgen Habermas, hold this belief in common: that the project of modernity is now deeply problematic.

Assailed though it is by pre-, anti- and postmodernists alike, modernism as a practice has not failed. On the contrary: modernism, at least as a tradition, has "won"—but its victory is a Pyrrhic one no different than defeat, for modernism is now largely absorbed. Originally oppositional, modernism defied the cultural order of the bourgeoisie and the "false normativity" (Habermas) of its history; today, however, it is the official culture. As Jameson notes, we entertain it: its once scandalous productions are in the university, in the museum, in the street. In short, modernism, as even Habermas writes, seems "dominant but dead."

This state of affairs suggests that if the modern project is to be saved at all, it must be exceeded. This is the imperative of much vital art of the present; it is also one incentive of this book. But how can we exceed the modern? How can we break with a program that makes a value of crisis (modernism), or progress beyond the era of Progress (modernity), or transgress the ideology of the transgressive (avant-gardism)? One can say, with Paul de Man, that every period suffers a "modern" moment, a moment of crisis or reckoning in which it becomes self-conscious *as* a period, but this is to view the modern ahistorically, almost as a category. True, the word may have "lost a fixed historical reference" (Habermas), but the ideology has not: modernism is a cultural construct based on specific conditions; it *has* a historical limit. And one motive of these essays is to trace this limit, to mark our change.

A first step, then, is to specify what modernity may be. Its project, Habermas writes, is one with that of the Enlightenment: to develop the spheres of science, morality and art "according to their inner logic." This program is still at work, say, in postwar or late modernism, with its stress on the purity of each art and the autonomy of culture as a whole. Rich though this disciplinary project once was—and urgent given the incursions of kitsch on one side and academe on the other—it nevertheless came to rarefy culture, to reify its forms—so much so that it provoked, at least in art, a counter-project in the form of an anarchic avant-garde (one thinks of dadaism and surrealism especially). This is the "modernism" that Habermas opposes to "the project of modernity" and dismisses as a negation of but one sphere: "Nothing remains from a desublimated meaning or a destructured form; an emancipatory effect does not follow."

Although repressed in late modernism, this "surrealist revolt" is returned in postmodernist art (or rather, its critique of representation is reaffirmed), for the mandate of postmodernism is also: "change the object itself." Thus, as Krauss writes, postmodernist practice "is not defined in relation to a given medium . . . but rather in relation to the logical operations on a set of cultural terms." In this way the very nature of art has changed; so too has the object of criticism: as Ulmer notes, a new "paraliterary" practice has come to the fore which dissolves the line between creative and critical forms. In the same way the old opposition of theory and practice is refused, especially, as Owens notes, by feminist artists for whom critical intervention is a tactical, political necessity. The discourse of knowledge is affected no less: in the midst of the academic disciplines, Jameson writes, extraordinary new projects have emerged. "Is the work of Michel Foucault, for example, to be called philosophy, history, social theory or political science?" (One may ask the same of the "literary criticism" of Jameson or Said.)

As the importance of a Foucault, a Jacques Derrida or a Roland Barthes attests, postmodernism is hard to conceive without continental theory, structuralism and poststructuralism in particular. Both have led us to reflect upon culture as a corpus of codes or myths (Barthes), as a set of imaginary resolutions to real contradictions (Claude Lévi-Strauss). In this light, a poem or picture is not necessarily privileged, and the artifact is likely to be treated less as a *work* in modernist terms—unique, symbolic, visionary— than as a *text* in a postmodernist sense—"already written," allegorical, contingent. With this textual model, one postmodernist strategy becomes clear: to deconstruct modernism not in order to seal it in its own image but in order to open it, to rewrite it; to open its closed systems (like the museum) to the "heterogeneity of texts" (Crimp), to rewrite its universal techniques in terms of "synthetic contradictions" (Frampton—in short, to challenge its master narratives with the "discourse of others" (Owens).

But this very plurality may be problematic: for if modernism consists of so many unique models (D.H. Lawrence, Marcel Proust . . .), then "there will be as many different forms of postmodernism as there were high modernisms in place, since the former are at least initially specific and local reactions *against* these models" (Jameson). As a result, these different forms might be reduced to indifference, or postmodernism dismissed as relativism (just as poststructuralism is dismissed as the absurd notion that nothing exists "outside the text"). This conflation, I think, should be guarded against, for postmodernism is not pluralism—the quixotic notion that all positions in culture and politics are now open and equal. This apocalyptic belief that anything goes, that the "end of ideology" is here, is simply the inverse of the fatalistic belief that nothing works, that we live under a "total system" without hope of redress—the very acquiescence that Ernest Mandel calls the "ideology of late capitalism."

Clearly, each position on or within postmodernism is marked by political "affiliations" (Said) and historical agendas. How we conceive postmodernism, then, is critical to how we represent both present and past—which aspects are stressed, which repressed. For what does it mean to periodize in terms of postmodernism: to argue that ours is an era of the death of the subject (Baudrillard) or of the loss of master narratives (Owens), to assert that we live in a consumer society that renders opposition difficult (Jameson) or amidst a mediocracy in which the humanities are marginal indeed (Said)? Such notions are not apocalyptic: they mark uneven developments, not clean breaks and new days. Perhaps, then, postmodernism is best conceived as a conflict of new and old modes—cultural and economic, the one not entirely autonomous, the other not all determinative—and of the interests vested therein. This at least makes the agenda of this book clear: to disengage the emergent cultural forms and social relations (Jameson) and to argue the import of doing so.

Even now, of course, there are standard positions to take on postmodernism: one may support postmodernism as populist and attack modernism as elitist or, conversely, support modernism as elitist—as culture proper—and attack postmodernism as mere kitsch. Such views reflect one thing: that postmodernism is publicly regarded (no doubt vis-à-vis postmodern architecture) as a necessary turn toward "tradition." Briefly, then, I want to sketch an oppositional postmodernism, the one which informs this book.

In cultural politics today, a basic opposition exists between a postmodernism which seeks to deconstruct modernism and resist the status quo and a postmodernism which repudiates the former to celebrate the latter: a postmodernism of resistance and a postmodernism of reaction. These essays deal mostly with the former—its desire to change the object and its social context. The postmodernism of reaction is far better known: though not monolithic, it is singular in its repudiation of modernism. This repudiation, voiced most shrilly perhaps by neoconservatives but echoed everywhere, is strategic: as Habermas cogently argues, the neoconservatives sever the cultural from the social, then blame the practices of the one (modernism) for the ills of the other (modernization). With cause and effect thus confounded, "adversary" culture is denounced even as the economic and political status quo is affirmed—indeed, a new "affirmative" culture is proposed.

Accordingly, culture remains a force but largely of social control, a gratuitous image drawn over the face of instrumentality (Frampton). Thus is this postmodernism conceived in therapeutic, not to say cosmetic, terms: as a return to the verities of tradition (in art, family, religion . . .). Modernism is reduced to a style (e.g., "formalism" or the International Style) and condemned, or excised entirely as a cultural mistake; pre- and postmodern elements are then elided, and the humanist tradition is preserved. But what is this return if not a resurrection of lost traditions set against modernism, a master plan imposed on a heterogeneous present?

A postmodernism of resistance, then, arises as a counter-practice not only to the official culture of modernism but also to the "false normativity" of a reactionary postmodernism. In opposition (but not *only* in opposition), a resistant postmodernism is concerned with a critical deconstruction of tradition, not an instrumental pastiche of pop- or pseudo- historical forms, with a critique of origins, not a return to them. In short, it seeks to question rather than exploit cultural codes, to explore rather than conceal social and political affiliations.

The essays that follow are diverse. Many subjects are discussed (architecture, sculpture, painting, photography, music, film . . .) but as practices transformed, not as ahistorical categories. So too many methods are engaged (structuralism and poststructuralism, Lacanian psychoanalysis, feminist criticism, Marxism . . .) but as models in conflict, not as sundry "approaches."

Jürgen Habermas poses the basic issues of a culture heir to the Enlightenment—of modernism and the avant-garde, of a progressive modernity and a reactionary postmodernity. He affirms the modern refusal of the "normative" but warns against "false negations;" at the same time, he denounces (neoconservative) antimodernism as reactionary. Opposed to both revolt and reaction, he calls for a critical reappropriation of the modern project.

In a sense, however, this critique belies the crisis—a crisis that Kenneth Frampton considers vis-à-vis modern architecture. The utopianism implicit in the Enlightenment and programmatic in modernism has led to catastrophe —the fabrics of non-Western cultures rent, the Western city reduced to the megapolis. Postmodern architects tend to respond superficially—with a populist "masking," a stylistic "avant-gardism" or a withdrawal into hermetic codes. Frampton calls instead for a critical mediation of the forms of modern civilization and of local culture, a mutual deconstruction of universal techniques and regional vernaculars.

The crisis of modernity was felt radically in the late 1950s and early '60s, the moment often cited as the postmodernist break and still the site of ideological conflict (mostly disavowal) today. If this crisis was experienced as a revolt of cultures without, it was no less marked by a rupture of culture within—even in its rarer realms, for example, in sculpture. Rosalind Krauss details how the logic of modern sculpture led in the '60s to its own deconstruction—and to the deconstruction of the modern order of the arts based on the Enlightenment order of distinct and autonomous disciplines. Today, she argues, "sculpture" exists as but one term in an "expanded field" of forms, all derived structurally. This, for Krauss, constitutes the postmodernist break: art conceived in terms of structure, not medium, oriented to "cultural terms."

Douglas Crimp also posits the existence of a break with modernism, specifically with its definition of the plane of representation. In the work of Robert Rauschenberg and others, the "natural," uniform surface of modernist painting is displaced, via photographic procedures, by the thoroughly cultural, textural site of the postmodernist picture. This aesthetic break, Crimp suggests, may signal an epistemological break with the very "table" or "archive" of modern knowledge. This he then explores vis-à-vis the modern institution of the museum, the authority of which rests on a representational conceit—a "science" of origins that does not hold up to scrutiny. Thus, he asserts, is the homogeneous series of works in the museum threatened, in postmodernism, by the heterogeneity of texts.

Craig Owens also regards postmodernism as a crisis in Western representation, its authority and universal claims—a crisis announced by heretofore marginal or repressed discourses, feminism most significant among them. As a radical critique of the master narratives of modern man, feminism, Owens argues, is a political and an epistemological event— political in that it challenges the order of patriarchal society, epistemological in that it questions the structure of its representations. This critique, he notes, is focused sharply in the contemporary practice of many woman artists, eight of whom he discusses.

The critique of representation is of course associated with poststructuralist theory, addressed here by Gregory Ulmer. Ulmer argues that criticism, its conventions of representation, are transformed today as the arts were at the advent of modernism. This transformation he details in terms of collage and montage (associated with various modernisms); deconstruction (specifically the critique of mimesis and the sign, associated with Jacques Derrida); and allegory (a form that attends to the historical materiality of thought, associated now with Walter Benjamin). These practices, Ulmer argues, have led to new cultural forms, examples of which are the writing of Roland Barthes and the composing of John Cage.

Fredric Jameson is less sanguine about the dissolution of the sign and the loss of representation. He notes, for example, that pastiche has become our ubiquitous mode (in film, especially), which suggests not only that we are awash in a sea of private languages but also that we wish to be recalled to times less problematic than our own. This in turn points to a refusal to engage the present or to think historically — a refusal that Jameson regards as characteristic of the "schizophrenia" of consumer society.

Jean Baudrillard also reflects upon our contemporary dissolution of public space and time. In a world of simulation, he writes, causality is lost: the object no longer serves as a mirror of the subject, and there is no longer a "scene," private or public — only "ob-scene" information. In effect, the self becomes a "schizo," a "pure screen . . . for all the networks of influence."

In a world so described, the very hope of resistance seems absurd: a resignation to which Edward Said objects. The status of information — or, for that matter, criticism — is hardly neutral: who benefits? And with this question he grounds these texts in the present context, "the Age of Reagan." To Said, the postmodern crossing of lines is mostly apparent: the cult of "the expert," the authority of "the field" still hold. Indeed, a "doctrine of noninterference" is tacitly assumed whereby "the humanities" and "politics" are held aloof from each other. But this only acts to rarefy the one and free the other, and to conceal the affiliations of both. As a result, the humanities come to serve in two ways: to disguise the unhumanistic operation of information and "to represent humane marginality." Here, then, we have come full circle: the Enlightenment, the disciplinary project of modernity, now mystifies; it makes for "religious constituencies," not "secular communities," and this abets state power. For Said (as for the Italian Marxist Antonio Gramsci) such power resides as much in civil institutions as in political and military ones. Thus, like Jameson, Said urges an awareness of the "hegemonic" aspects of cultural texts and proposes a counter-practice of interference. Here (in solidarity with Frampton, Owens, Ulmer . . .), he cites these strategies: a critique of official representations, alternative uses of informational modes (like photography), and a recovery of (the history of) others.

Though diverse, these essays share many concerns: a critique of Western representation(s) and modern "supreme fictions"; a desire to think in terms sensitive to difference (of others without opposition, of heterogeneity without hierarchy); a skepticism regarding autonomous "spheres" of culture or separate "fields" of experts; an imperative to go beyond formal filiations (of text to text) to trace social affiliations (the institutional "density" of the text in the world); in short, a will to grasp the present nexus of culture and politics and to affirm a practice resistant both to academic modernism and political reaction.

These concerns are signalled here by the rubric "anti-aesthetic," which is *not* intended as one more assertion of the negation of art or of representation as such. It was modernism that was marked by such "negations," espoused in the anarchic hope of an "emancipatory effect" or in the utopian dream of a time of pure presence, a space beyond representation. This is not the case here: all these critics take for granted that we are never outside representation—or rather, never outside its politics. Here then, "anti-aesthetic" is the sign not of a modern nihilism—which so often transgressed the law only to confirm it—but rather of a critique which destructures the order of representations in order to reinscribe them.

"Anti-aesthetic" also signals that the very notion of the aesthetic, its network of ideas, is in question here: the idea that aesthetic experience exists apart, without "purpose," all but beyond history, or that art can now effect a world at once (inter)subjective, concrete and universal—a symbolic totality. Like "postmodernism," then, "anti-aesthetic" marks a cultural position on the present: are categories afforded by the aesthetic still valid? (For example, is the model of subjective taste not threatened by mass mediation, or that of universal vision by the rise of other cultures?) More locally, "anti-aesthetic" also signals a practice, cross-disciplinary in nature, that is sensitive to cultural forms engaged in a politic (e.g., feminist art) or rooted in a vernacular—that is, to forms that deny the idea of a privileged aesthetic realm.

The adventures of the aesthetic make up one of the great narratives of modernity: from the time of its autonomy through art-for-art's-sake to its status as a necessary negative category, a critique of the world as it is. It is this last moment (figured brilliantly in the writings of Theodor Adorno) that is hard to relinquish: the notion of the aesthetic as subversive, a critical interstice in an otherwise instrumental world. Now, however, we have to consider that this aesthetic space too is eclipsed—or rather, that its criticality is now largely illusory (and so instrumental). In such an event, the strategy of an Adorno, of "negative commitment," might have to be revised or rejected, and a new strategy of interference (associated with Gramsci) devised. This, at least, is the thrust of the essays in this book. Such a strategy, of course, remains romantic if it is not aware of its own limits, which in the present world are strict indeed. And yet this much is clear: in the face of a culture of reaction on all sides, a practice of resistance is needed.

Modernity — An Incomplete Project

JÜRGEN HABERMAS

In 1980, architects were admitted to the Biennial in Venice, following painters and filmmakers. The note sounded at this first Architecture Biennial was one of disappointment. I would describe it by saying that those who exhibited in Venice formed an avant-garde of reversed fronts. I mean that they sacrificed the tradition of modernity in order to make room for a new historicism. Upon this occasion, a critic of the German newspaper, *Frankfurter Allgemeine Zeitung,* advanced a thesis whose significance reaches beyond this particular event; it is a diagnosis of our times: "Postmodernity definitely presents itself as Antimodernity." This statement describes an emotional current of our times which has penetrated all spheres of intellectual life. It has placed on the agenda theories of postenlightenment, postmodernity, even of posthistory.

From history we know the phrase, "The Ancients and the Moderns." Let me begin by defining these concepts. The term "modern" has a long history, one which has been investigated by Hans Robert Jauss.[1] The word "modern" in its Latin form "modernus" was used for the first time in the late 5th century in order to distinguish the present, which had become officially Christian, from the Roman and pagan past. With varying content, the term "modern" again and again expresses the consciousness of an epoch that relates itself to the past of antiquity, in order to view itself as the result of a transition from the old to the new.

Some writers restrict this concept of "modernity" to the Renaissance, but this is historically too narrow. People considered themselves modern during

This essay was originally delivered as a talk in September 1980 when Habermas was awarded the Theodor W. Adorno prize by the city of Frankfurt. It was subsequently delivered as a James Lecture of the New York Institute for the Humanities at New York University in March 1981 and published under the title "Modernity Versus Postmodernity" in *New German Critique* 22 (Winter, 1981). It is reprinted here by permission of the author and the publisher.

the period of Charles the Great in the 12th century, as well as in France of the late 17th century at the time of the famous "Querelle des Anciens et des Modernes." That is to say, the term "modern" appeared and reappeared exactly during those periods in Europe when the consciousness of a new epoch formed itself through a renewed relationship to the ancients — whenever, moreover, antiquity was considered a model to be recovered through some kind of imitation.

The spell which the classics of the ancient world cast upon the spirit of later times was first dissolved with the ideals of the French Enlightenment. Specifically, the idea of being "modern" by looking back to the ancients changed with the belief, inspired by modern science, in the infinite progress of knowledge and in the infinite advance towards social and moral betterment. Another form of modernist consciousness was formed in the wake of this change. The romantic modernist sought to oppose the antique ideals of the classicists; he looked for a new historical epoch and found it in the idealized Middle Ages. However, this new ideal age, established early in the 19th century, did not remain a fixed ideal. In the course of the 19th century, there emerged out of this romantic spirit that radicalized consciousness of modernity which freed itself from all specific historical ties. This most recent modernism simply makes an abstract opposition between tradition and the present; and we are, in a way, still the contemporaries of that kind of aesthetic modernity which first appeared in the midst of the 19th century. Since then, the distinguishing mark of works which count as modern is "the new" which will be overcome and made obsolete through the novelty of the next style. But, while that which is merely "stylish" will soon become outmoded, that which is modern preserves a secret tie to the classical. Of course, whatever can survive time has always been considered to be a classic. But the emphatically modern document no longer borrows this power of being a classic from the authority of a past epoch; instead, a modern work becomes a classic because it has once been authentically modern. Our sense of modernity creates its own self-enclosed canons of being classic. In this sense we speak, e.g., in view of the history of modern art, of classical modernity. The relation between "modern" and "classical" has definitely lost a fixed historical reference.

The Discipline of Aesthetic Modernity

The spirit and discipline of aesthetic modernity assumed clear contours in the work of Baudelaire. Modernity then unfolded in various avant-garde movements and finally reached its climax in the Café Voltaire of the dadaists and in surrealism. Aesthetic modernity is characterized by attitudes which find a common focus in a changed consciousness of time. This time consciousness expresses itself through metaphors of the vanguard and the avant-garde. The avant-garde understands itself as invading unknown territory, exposing itself to the dangers of sudden, shocking encounters, conquering an as yet unoccupied future. The avant-garde must find a direction in a landscape into which no one seems to have yet ventured.

But these forward gropings, this anticipation of an undefined future and the cult of the new mean in fact the exaltation of the present. The new time consciousness, which enters philosophy in the writings of Bergson, does more than express the experience of mobility in society, of acceleration in history, of discontinuity in everyday life. The new value placed on the transitory, the elusive and the ephemeral, the very celebration of dynamism, discloses a longing for an undefiled, immaculate and stable present.

This explains the rather abstract language in which the modernist temper has spoken of the "past." Individual epochs lose their distinct forces. Historical memory is replaced by the heroic affinity of the present with the extremes of history—a sense of time wherein decadence immediately recognizes itself in the barbaric, the wild and the primitive. We observe the anarchistic intention of blowing up the continuum of history, and we can account for it in terms of the subversive force of this new aesthetic consciousness. Modernity revolts against the normalizing functions of tradition; modernity lives on the experience of rebelling against all that is normative. This revolt is one way to neutralize the standards of both morality and utility. This aesthetic consciousness continuously stages a dialectical play between secrecy and public scandal; it is addicted to a fascination with that horror which accompanies the act of profaning, and yet is always in flight from the trivial results of profanation.

On the other hand, the time consciousness articulated in avant-garde art is not simply ahistorical; it is directed against what might be called a false normativity in history. The modern, avant-garde spirit has sought to use the past in a different way; it disposes those pasts which have been made available by the objectifying scholarship of historicism, but it opposes at the same time a neutralized history which is locked up in the museum of historicism.

Drawing upon the spirit of surrealism, Walter Benjamin constructs the relationship of modernity to history in what I would call a posthistoricist attitude. He reminds us of the self-understanding of the French Revolution: "The Revolution cited ancient Rome, just as fashion cites an antiquated dress. Fashion has a scent for what is current, whenever this moves within the thicket of what was once." This is Benjamin's concept of the *Jetztzeit,* of the present as a moment of revelation; a time in which splinters of a messianic presence are enmeshed. In this sense, for Robespierre, the antique Rome was a past laden with momentary revelations.[2]

Now, this spirit of aesthetic modernity has recently begun to age. It has been recited once more in the 1960s; after the 1970s, however, we must admit to ourselves that this modernism arouses a much fainter response today than it did fifteen years ago. Octavio Paz, a fellow-traveller of modernity, noted already in the middle of the 1960s that "the avant-garde of 1967 repeats the deeds and gestures of those of 1917. We are experiencing the end of the idea of modern art." The work of Peter Bürger has since taught us to speak of "post-avant-garde" art; this term is chosen to indicate the failure of the surrealist rebellion.[3] But what is the meaning of this failure? Does it signal a farewell to modernity? Thinking more generally, does the existence of a post-avant-garde mean there is a transition to that broader phenomenon called postmodernity?

This is in fact how Daniel Bell, the most brilliant of the American neoconservatives, interprets matters. In his book, *The Cultural Contradictions of Capitalism,* Bell argues that the crises of the developed societies of the West are to be traced back to a split between culture and society. Modernist culture has come to penetrate the values of everyday life; the life-world is infected by modernism. Because of the forces of modernism, the principle of unlimited self-realization, the demand for authentic self-experience and the subjectivism of a hyperstimulated sensitivity have come to be dominant. This temperament unleashes hedonistic motives irreconcilable with the discipline of professional life in society, Bell says. Moreover, modernist culture is altogether incompatible with the moral basis of a purposive, rational conduct of life. In this manner, Bell places the burden of responsibility for the dissolution of the Protestant ethic (a phenomenon which had already disturbed Max Weber) on the "adversary culture." Culture in its modern form stirs up hatred against the conventions and virtues of everyday life, which has become rationalized under the pressures of economic and administrative imperatives.

I would call your attention to a complex wrinkle in this view. The impulse of modernity, we are told on the other hand, is exhausted; anyone who considers himself avant-garde can read his own death warrant. Although the avant-garde is still considered to be expanding, it is supposedly no longer creative. Modernism is dominant but dead. For the neoconservative the question then arises: how can norms arise in society which will limit libertinism, reestablish the ethic of discipline and work? What new norms will put a brake on the levelling caused by the social welfare state so that the virtues of individual competition for achievement can again dominate? Bell sees a religious revival to be the only solution. Religious faith tied to a faith in tradition will provide individuals with clearly defined identities and existential security.

Cultural Modernity and Societal Modernization

One can certainly not conjure up by magic the compelling beliefs which command authority. Analyses like Bell's, therefore, only result in an attitude which is spreading in Germany no less than in the States: an intellectual and political confrontation with the carriers of cultural modernity. I cite Peter Steinfels, an observer of the new style which the neoconservatives have imposed upon the intellectual scene in the 1970s:

> The struggle takes the form of exposing every manifestation of what could be considered an oppositionist mentality and tracing its "logic" so as to link it to various forms of extremism: drawing the connection between modernism and nihilism...between government regulation and totalitarianism, between criticism of arms expenditures and subservience to communism, between Women's liberation or homosexual rights and the destruction of the family... between the Left generally and terrorism, anti-semitism, and fascism...[4]

The *ad hominem* approach and the bitterness of these intellectual accusations have also been trumpeted loudly in Germany. They should not be explained so much in terms of the psychology of neoconservative writers; rather, they are rooted in the analytical weaknesses of neoconservative doctrine itself.

Neoconservatism shifts onto cultural modernism the uncomfortable burdens of a more or less successful capitalist modernization of the economy and society. The neoconservative doctrine blurs the relationship between the welcomed process of societal modernization on the one hand, and the lamented cultural development on the other. The neoconservative does not uncover the economic and social causes for the altered attitudes towards work, consumption, achievement and leisure. Consequently, he attributes all of the following—hedonism, the lack of social identification, the lack of obedience, narcissism, the withdrawal from status and achievement competition—to the domain of "culture." In fact, however, culture is intervening in the creation of all these problems in only a very indirect and mediated fashion.

In the neoconservative view, those intellectuals who still feel themselves committed to the project of modernity are then presented as taking the place of those unanalyzed causes. The mood which feeds neoconservatism today in no way originates from discontent about the antinomian consequences of a culture breaking from the museums into the stream of ordinary life. This discontent has not been called into life by modernist intellectuals. It is rooted in deep-seated reactions against the process of *societal* modernization. Under the pressures of the dynamics of economic growth and the organizational accomplishments of the state, this social modernization penetrates deeper and deeper into previous forms of human existence. I would describe this subordination of the life-worlds under the system's imperatives as a matter of disturbing the communicative infrastructure of everyday life.

Thus, for example, neopopulist protests only express in pointed fashion a widespread fear regarding the destruction of the urban and natural environment and of forms of human sociability. There is a certain irony about these protests in terms of neoconservatism. The tasks of passing on a cultural tradition, of social integration and of socialization require adherence to what I call communicative rationality. But the occasions for protest and discontent originate precisely when spheres of communicative action, centered on the reproduction and transmission of values and norms, are penetrated by a form of modernization guided by standards of economic and administrative rationality—in other words, by standards of rationalization quite different from those of communicative rationality on which those spheres depend. But neoconservative doctrines turn our attention precisely away from such societal processes: they project the causes, which they do not bring to light, onto the plane of a subversive culture and its advocates.

To be sure, cultural modernity generates its own aporias as well. Independently from the consequences of *societal* modernization and within the perspective of *cultural* development itself, there originate motives for doubting the project of modernity. Having dealt with a feeble kind of criticism of modernity—that of neoconservatism—let me now move our discussion of modernity and its discontents into a different domain that touches on these aporias of cultural modernity—issues that often serve only as a pretense for those positions which either call for a postmodernity, recommend a return to some form of premodernity, or throw modernity radically overboard.

The Project of Enlightenment

The idea of modernity is intimately tied to the development of European art, but what I call "the project of modernity" comes only into focus when we dispense with the usual concentration upon art. Let me start a different analysis by recalling an idea from Max Weber. He characterized cultural modernity as the separation of the substantive reason expressed in religion and metaphysics into three autonomous spheres. They are: science, morality and art. These came to be differentiated because the unified world-views of religion and metaphysics fell apart. Since the 18th century, the problems inherited from these older world-views could be arranged so as to fall under specific aspects of validity: truth, normative rightness, authenticity and beauty. They could then be handled as questions of knowledge, or of justice and morality, or of taste. Scientific discourse, theories of morality, jurisprudence, and the production and criticism of art could in turn be institutionalized. Each domain of culture could be made to correspond to cultural professions in which problems could be dealt with as the concern of special experts. This professionalized treatment of the cultural tradition brings to the fore the intrinsic structures of each of the three dimensions of culture. There appear the structures of cognitive-instrumental, of moral-practical and of aesthetic-expressive rationality, each of these under the control of specialists who seem more adept at being logical in these particular ways than other people are. As a result, the distance grows between the culture of the experts and that of the larger public. What accrues to culture through specialized treatment and reflection does not immediately and necessarily become the property of everyday praxis. With cultural rationalization of this sort, the threat increases that the life-world, whose traditional substance has already been devalued, will become more and more impoverished.

The project of modernity formulated in the 18th century by the philosophers of the Enlightenment consisted in their efforts to develop objective science, universal morality and law, and autonomous art according to their inner logic. At the same time, this project intended to release the cognitive potentials of each of these domains from their esoteric forms. The Enlightenment philosophers wanted to utilize this accumulation of specialized culture for the enrichment of everyday life—that is to say, for the rational organization of everyday social life.

Enlightenment thinkers of the cast of mind of Condorcet still had the extravagant expectation that the arts and sciences would promote not only the control of natural forces but also understanding of the world and of the self, moral progress, the justice of institutions and even the happiness of human beings. The 20th century has shattered this optimism. The differentiation of science, morality and art has come to mean the autonomy of the segments treated by the specialist and their separation from the hermeneutics of everyday communication. This splitting off is the problem that has given rise to efforts to "negate" the culture of expertise. But the problem won't go away: should we try to hold on to the *intentions* of the Enlightenment, feeble as they may be, or should we declare the entire project of modernity a lost cause? I now want to return to the problem of artistic culture, having explained why, historically, aesthetic modernity is only a part of cultural modernity in general.

The False Programs of the Negation of Culture

Greatly oversimplifying, I would say that in the history of modern art one can detect a trend towards ever greater autonomy in the definition and practice of art. The category of "beauty" and the domain of beautiful objects were first constituted in the Renaissance. In the course of the 18th century, literature, the fine arts and music were institutionalized as activities independent from sacred and courtly life. Finally, around the middle of the 19th century an aestheticist conception of art emerged, which encouraged the artist to produce his work according to the distinct consciousness of art for art's sake. The autonomy of the aesthetic sphere could then become a deliberate project: the talented artist could lend authentic expression to those experiences he had in encountering his own de-centered subjectivity, detached from the constraints of routinized cognition and everyday action.

In the mid-19th century, in painting and literature, a movement began which Octavio Paz finds epitomized already in the art criticism of Baudelaire. Color, lines, sounds and movement ceased to serve primarily the cause of representation; the media of expression and the techniques of production themselves became the aesthetic object. Theodor W. Adorno could therefore begin his *Aesthetic Theory* with the following sentence: "It is now taken for granted that nothing which concerns art can be taken for granted any more: neither art itself, nor art in its relationship to the whole, nor even the right of art to exist." And this is what surrealism then denied: *das Existenzrecht der Kunst als Kunst*. To be sure, surrealism would not have challenged the right of art to exist, if modern art no longer had advanced a promise of happiness concerning its own relationship "to the whole" of life. For Schiller, such a promise was delivered by aesthetic intuition, but not fulfilled by it. Schiller's *Letters on the Aesthetic Education of Man* speaks to us of a utopia reaching beyond art itself. But by the time of Baudelaire, who repeated this *promesse de bonheur* via art, the utopia of reconciliation with society had gone sour. A relation of opposites had come into being; art had become a critical mirror, showing the irreconcilable nature of the aesthetic and the social worlds. This modernist transformation was all the more painfully realized, the more art alienated itself from life and withdrew into the untouchableness of complete autonomy. Out of such emotional currents finally gathered those explosive energies which unloaded in the surrealist attempt to blow up the autarkical sphere of art and to force a reconciliation of art and life.

But all those attempts to level art and life, fiction and praxis, appearance and reality to one plane; the attempts to remove the distinction between artifact and object of use, between conscious staging and spontaneous excitement; the attempts to declare everything to be art and everyone to be an artist, to retract all criteria and to equate aesthetic judgment with the expression of subjective experiences—all these undertakings have proved themselves to be sort of nonsense experiments. These experiments have served to bring back to life, and to illuminate all the more glaringly, exactly those structures of art which they were meant to dissolve. They gave a new legitimacy, as ends in themselves, to appearance as the medium of fiction, to the transcendence of the artwork over society, to the concentrated and planned character of artistic production as well as to the special cognitive status of judgments of taste. The radical attempt to negate art has ended up ironically by giving due exactly to these categories through which Enlightenment aesthetics had circumscribed its object domain. The surrealists waged the most extreme warfare, but two mistakes in particular destroyed their revolt. First, when the containers of an autonomously developed cultural sphere are shattered, the contents get dispersed. Nothing remains from a desublimated meaning or a destructured form; an emancipatory effect does not follow.

Their second mistake has more important consequences. In everyday communication, cognitive meanings, moral expectations, subjective expressions and evaluations must relate to one another. Communication processes need a cultural tradition covering all spheres—cognitive, moral-practical and expressive. A rationalized everyday life, therefore, could hardly be saved from cultural impoverishment through breaking open a single cultural sphere—art—and so providing access to just one of the specialized knowledge complexes. The surrealist revolt would have replaced only one abstraction.

In the spheres of theoretical knowledge and morality, there are parallels to this failed attempt of what we might call the false negation of culture. Only they are less pronounced. Since the days of the Young Hegelians, there has been talk about the negation of philosophy. Since Marx, the question of the relationship of theory and practice has been posed. However, Marxist intellectuals joined a social movement; and only at its peripheries were there sectarian attempts to carry out a program of the negation of philosophy similar to the surrealist program to negate art. A parallel to the surrealist mistakes becomes visible in these programs when one observes the consequences of dogmatism and of moral rigorism.

A reified everyday praxis can be cured only by creating unconstrained interaction of the cognitive with the moral-practical and the aesthetic-expressive elements. Reification cannot be overcome by forcing just one of those highly stylized cultural spheres to open up and become more accessible. Instead, we see under certain circumstances a relationship emerge between terroristic activities and the over-extension of any one of these spheres into other domains: examples would be tendencies to aestheticize politics, or to replace politics by moral rigorism or to submit it to the dogmatism of a doctrine. These phenomena should not lead us, however, into denouncing the intentions of the surviving Enlightenment tradition as intentions rooted in a "terroristic reason."[5] Those who lump together the very project of modernity with the state of consciousness and the spectacular action of the individual terrorist are no less short-sighted than those who would claim that the incomparably more persistent and extensive bureaucratic terror practiced in the dark, in the cellars of the military and secret police, and in camps and institutions, is the *raison d'être* of the modern state, only because this kind of administrative terror makes use of the coercive means of modern bureaucracies.

Alternatives

I think that instead of giving up modernity and its project as a lost cause, we should learn from the mistakes of those extravagant programs which have tried to negate modernity. Perhaps the types of reception of art may offer an example which at least indicates the direction of a way out.

Bourgeois art had two expectations at once from its audiences. On the one hand, the layman who enjoyed art should educate himself to become an expert. On the other hand, he should also behave as a competent consumer who uses art and relates aesthetic experiences to his own life problems. This second, and seemingly harmless, manner of experiencing art has lost its radical implications exactly because it had a confused relation to the attitude of being expert and professional.

To be sure, artistic production would dry up, if it were not carried out in the form of a specialized treatment of autonomous problems and if it were to cease to be the concern of experts who do not pay so much attention to exoteric questions. Both artists and critics accept thereby the fact that such problems fall under the spell of what I earlier called the "inner logic" of a cultural domain. But this sharp delineation, this exclusive concentration on one aspect of validity alone and the exclusion of aspects of truth and justice, break down as soon as aesthetic experience is drawn into an individual life history and is absorbed into ordinary life. The reception of art by the layman, or by the "everyday expert," goes in a rather different direction than the reception of art by the professional critic.

Albrecht Wellmer has drawn my attention to one way that an aesthetic experience which is not framed around the experts' critical judgments of taste can have its significance altered: as soon as such an experience is used to illuminate a life-historical situation and is related to life problems, it enters into a language game which is no longer that of the aesthetic critic. The aesthetic experience then not only renews the interpretation of our needs in whose light we perceive the world. It permeates as well our cognitive significations and our normative expectations and changes the manner in which all these moments refer to one another. Let me give an example of this process.

This manner of receiving and relating to art is suggested in the first volume of the work *The Aesthetics of Resistance* by the German-Swedish writer Peter Weiss. Weiss describes the process of reappropriating art by presenting a group of politically motivated, knowledge-hungry workers in 1937 in Berlin.[6] These were young people who, through an evening high-school education, acquired the intellectual means to fathom the general and social history of European art. Out of the resilient edifice of this objective mind, embodied in works of art which they saw again and again in the museums in Berlin, they started removing their own chips of stone, which they gathered together and reassembled in the context of their own milieu. This milieu was far removed from that of traditional education as well as from the then existing regime. These young workers went back and forth between the edifice of European art and their own milieu until they were able to illuminate both.

In examples like this which illustrate the reappropriation of the expert's culture from the standpoint of the life-world, we can discern an element which does justice to the intentions of the hopeless surrealist revolts, perhaps even more to Brecht's and Benjamin's interests in how art works, which having lost their aura, could yet be received in illuminating ways. In sum, the project of modernity has not yet been fulfilled. And the reception of art is only one of at least three of its aspects. The project aims at a differentiated relinking of modern culture with an everyday praxis that still depends on vital heritages, but would be impoverished through mere traditionalism. This new connection, however, can only be established under the condition that societal modernization will also be steered in a different direction. The life-world has to become able to develop institutions out of itself which set limits to the internal dynamics and imperatives of an almost autonomous economic system and its administrative complements.

If I am not mistaken, the chances for this today are not very good. More or less in the entire Western world a climate has developed that furthers capitalist modernization processes as well as trends critical of cultural modernism. The disillusionment with the very failures of those programs that called for the negation of art and philosophy has come to serve as a pretense for conservative positions. Let me briefly distinguish the anti-modernism of the "young conservatives" from the premodernism of the "old conservatives" and from the postmodernism of the neoconservatives.

The "young conservatives" recapitulate the basic experience of aesthetic modernity. They claim as their own the revelations of a decentered subjectivity, emancipated from the imperatives of work and usefulness, and with this experience they step outside the modern world. On the basis of modernistic attitudes they justify an irreconcilable antimodernism. They remove into the sphere of the far-away and the archaic the spontaneous powers of imagination, self-experience and emotion. To instrumental reason they juxtapose in Manichean fashion a principle only accessible through evocation, be it the will to power or sovereignty, Being or the Dionysiac force of the poetical. In France this line leads from Georges Bataille via Michel Foucault to Jacques Derrida.

The "old conservatives" do not allow themselves to be contaminated by cultural modernism. They observe the decline of substantive reason, the differentiation of science, morality and art, the modern world view and its merely procedural rationality, with sadness and recommend a withdrawal to a position *anterior* to modernity. Neo-Aristotelianism, in particular, enjoys a certain success today. In view of the problematic of ecology, it allows itself to call for a cosmological ethic. (As belonging to this school, which originates with Leo Strauss, one can count the interesting works of Hans Jonas and Robert Spaemann.)

Finally, the neoconservatives welcome the development of modern science, as long as this only goes beyond its sphere to carry forward technical progress, capitalist growth and rational administration. Moreover, they recommend a politics of defusing the explosive content of cultural modernity. According to one thesis, science, when properly understood, has become irrevocably meaningless for the orientation of the life-world. A further thesis is that politics must be kept as far aloof as possible from the demands of moral-practical justification. And a third thesis asserts the pure immanence of art, disputes that it has a utopian content, and points to its illusory character in order to limit the aesthetic experience to privacy. (One could name here the early Wittgenstein, Carl Schmitt of the middle period, and Gottfried Benn of the late period.) But with the decisive confinement of science, morality and art to autonomous spheres separated from the life-world and administered by experts, what remains from the project of cultural modernity is only what we would have if we were to give up the project of modernity altogether. As a replacement one points to traditions which, however, are held to be immune to demands of (normative) justification and validation.

This typology is like any other, of course, a simplification, but it may not prove totally useless for the analysis of contemporary intellectual and political confrontations. I fear that the ideas of antimodernity, together with an additional touch of premodernity, are becoming popular in the circles of alternative culture. When one observes the transformations of consciousness within political parties in Germany, a new ideological shift *(Tendenzwende)* becomes visible. And this is the alliance of postmodernists with premodernists. It seems to me that there is no party in particular that monopolizes the abuse of intellectuals and the position of neoconservatism. I therefore have good reason to be thankful for the liberal spirit in which the city of Frankfurt offers me a prize bearing the name of Theodor Adorno, a most significant son of this city, who as philosopher and writer has stamped the image of the intellectual in our country in incomparable fashion, who, even more, has become the very image of emulation for the intellectual.

Translated by Seyla Ben-Habib

References

1. Jauss is a prominent German literary historian and critic involved in "the aesthetics of reception," a type of criticism related to reader-response criticism in this country. For a discussion of "modern" see Jauss, *Asthetische Normen und geschichtliche Reflexion in der Querelle des Anciens et des Modernes* (Munich, 1964). For a reference in English see Jauss, "History of Art and Pragmatic History," *Toward an Aesthetic of Reception,* trans. Timothy Bahti (Minneapolis: University of Minnesota Press, 1982), pp. 46-8. [Ed.]
2. See Benjamin, "Theses on the Philosophy of History," *Illuminations,* trans. Harry Zohn (New York: Schocken, 1969), p. 261. [Ed.]
3. For Paz on the avant-garde see in particular *Children of the Mire: Modern Poetry from Romanticism to the Avant-Garde* (Cambridge: Harvard University Press, 1974), pp. 148-64. For Bürger see *Theory of the Avant-Garde* (Minneapolis: University of Minnesota Press, Fall 1983). [Ed.]
4. Peter Steinfels, *The Neoconservatives* (New York: Simon and Schuster, 1979), p. 65.
5. The phrase "to aestheticize politics" echoes Benjamin's famous formulation of the false social program of the fascists in "The Work of Art in the Age of Mechanical Reproduction." Habermas's criticism here of Enlightenment critics seems directed less at Adorno and Max Horkheimer than at the contemporary *nouveaux philosophes* (Bernard-Henri Lèvy, etc.) and their German and American counterparts. [Ed.]
6. The reference is to the novel *Die Asthetik des Widerstands* (1975-8) by the author perhaps best known here for his 1965 play *Marat/Sade.* The work of art "reappropriated" by the workers is the Pergamon altar, emblem of power, classicism and rationality. [Ed.]

Towards a Critical Regionalism:
Six Points for an Architecture of Resistance

KENNETH FRAMPTON

The phenomenon of universalization, while being an advancement of man-kind, at the same time constitutes a sort of subtle destruction, not only of traditional cultures, which might not be an irreparable wrong, but also of what I shall call for the time being the creative nucleus of great cultures, that nucleus on the basis of which we interpret life, what I shall call in advance the ethical and mythical nucleus of mankind. The conflict springs up from there. We have the feeling that this single world civilization at the same time exerts a sort of attrition or wearing away at the expense of the cultural resources which have made the great civilizations of the past. This threat is expressed, among other disturbing effects, by the spreading before our eyes of a mediocre civilization which is the absurd counterpart of what I was just calling elementary culture. Everywhere throughout the world, one finds the same bad movie, the same slot machines, the same plastic or aluminum atrocities, the same twisting of language by propaganda, etc. It seems as if mankind, by approaching en masse *a basic consumer culture, were also stopped* en masse *at a subcultural level. Thus we come to the crucial problem confronting nations just rising from underdevelopment. In order to get on to the road toward modernization, is it necessary to jettison the old cultural past which has been the* raison d'être *of a nation? ...Whence the paradox: on the one hand, it has to root itself in the soil of its past, forge a national spirit, and unfurl this spiritual and cultural revindication before the colonialist's personality. But in order to take part in modern civilization, it is necessary at the same time to take part in scientific, technical, c id political rationality, something which very often requires the pure and simple abandon of a whole cultural past. It is a fact: every culture cannot sustain and absorb the shock of modern civilization. There is the paradox: how to become n. dern and to return to sources; how to revive an old, dormant civilization and ake part in universal civilization.*[1]

—Paul Ricoeur, *History and Truth*

1. Culture and Civilization

Modern building is now so universally conditioned by optimized technology that the possibility of creating significant urban form has become extremely limited. The restrictions jointly imposed by automotive distribution and the volatile play of land speculation serve to limit the scope of urban design to such a degree that any intervention tends to be reduced either to the manipulation of elements predetermined by the imperatives of production, or to a kind of superficial masking which modern development requires for the facilitation of marketing and the maintenance of social control. Today the practice of architecture seems to be increasingly polarized between, on the one hand, a so-called "high-tech" approach predicated exclusively upon production and, on the other, the provision of a "compensatory facade" to cover up the harsh realities of this universal system.[2]

Twenty years ago the dialectical interplay between civilization and culture still afforded the possibility of maintaining some general control over the shape and significance of the urban fabric. The last two decades, however, have radically transformed the metropolitan centers of the developed world. What were still essentially 19th-century city fabrics in the early 1960s have since become progressively overlaid by the two symbiotic instruments of Megalopolitan development—the freestanding high-rise and the serpentine freeway. The former has finally come into its own as the prime device for realizing the increased land value brought into being by the latter. The typical downtown which, up to twenty years ago, still presented a mixture of residential stock with tertiary and secondary industry has now become little more than a *burolandschaft* city-scape: the victory of universal civilization over locally inflected culture. The predicament posed by Ricoeur—namely, "how to become modern and to return to sources"[3]—now seems to be circumvented by the apocalyptic thrust of modernization, while the ground in which the mytho-ethical nucleus of a society might take root has become eroded by the rapacity of development.[4]

Ever since the beginning of the Enlightenment, *civilization* has been primarily concerned with instrumental reason, while *culture* has addressed itself to the specifics of expression—to the realization of the being and the evolution of its *collective* psycho-social reality. Today civilization tends to be increasingly embroiled in a never-ending chain of "means and ends" wherein, according to Hannah Arendt, "The 'in order to' has become the content of the 'for the sake of;' utility established as meaning generates meaninglessness."[5]

2. The Rise and Fall of the Avant-Garde

The emergence of the avant-garde is inseparable from the modernization of both society and architecture. Over the past century-and-a-half avant-garde culture has assumed different roles, at times facilitating the process of modernization and thereby acting, in part, as a progressive, liberative form, at times being virulently opposed to the positivism of bourgeois culture. By and large, avant-garde architecture has played a positive role with regard to the progressive trajectory of the Enlightenment. Exemplary of this is the role played by Neoclassicism: from the mid-18th century onwards it serves as both a symbol of and an instrument for the propagation of universal civilization. The mid-19th century, however, saw the historical avant-garde assume an adversary stance towards both industrial process and Neoclassical form. This is the first concerted reaction on the part of "tradition" to the process of modernization as the Gothic Revival and the Arts-and-Crafts movements take up a categorically negative attitude towards both utilitarian-ism and the division of labor. Despite this critique, modernization continues unabated, and throughout the last half of the 19th century bourgeois art distances itself progressively from the harsh realities of colonialism and paleo-technological exploitation. Thus at the end of the century the avant-gardist Art Nouveau takes refuge in the compensatory thesis of "art for art's sake," retreating to nostalgic or phantasmagoric dream-worlds inspired by the cathartic hermeticism of Wagner's music-drama.

The progressive avant-garde emerges in full force, however, soon after the turn of the century with the advent of Futurism. This unequivocal critique of the *ancien régime* gives rise to the primary positive cultural formations of the 1920s: to Purism, Neoplasticism and Constructivism. These movements are the last occasion on which radical avant-gardism is able to identify itself wholeheartedly with the process of modernization. In the immediate aftermath of World War I—"the war to end all wars"—the triumphs of science, medicine and industry seemed to confirm the liberative promise of the modern project. In the 1930s, however, the prevailing backwardness and chronic insecurity of the newly urbanized masses, the upheavals caused by war, revolution and economic depression, followed by a sudden and crucial need for psycho-social stability in the face of global political and economic crises, all induce a state of affairs in which the interests of both monopoly and state capitalism are, for the first time in modern history, divorced from the liberative drives of cultural moderniza-tion. Universal civilization and world culture cannot be drawn upon to sustain "the myth of the State," and one reaction-formation succeeds another as the historical avant-garde founders on the rocks of the Spanish Civil War.

Not least among these reactions is the reassertion of Neo-Kantian aesthetics as a substitute for the culturally liberative modern project. Confused by the political and cultural politics of Stalinism, former left-wing protagonists of socio-cultural modernization now recommend a strategic withdrawal from the project of totally transforming the existing reality. This renunciation is predicated on the belief that as long as the struggle between socialism and capitalism persists (with the manipulative mass-culture politics that this conflict necessarily entails), the modern world cannot continue to entertain the prospect of evolving a marginal, liberative, avant-gardist culture which would break (or speak of the break) with the history of bourgeois repression. Close to *l'art pour l'art,* this position was first advanced as a "holding pattern" in Clement Greenberg's "Avant-Garde and Kitsch" of 1939; this essay concludes somewhat ambiguously with the words: "Today we look to socialism *simply* for the preservation of whatever living culture we have right now." [6] Greenberg reformulated this position in specifically formalist terms in his essay "Modernist Painting" of 1965, wherein he wrote:

> Having been denied by the Enlightenment of all tasks they could take seriously, they [the arts] looked as though they were going to be assimilated to entertainment pure and simple, and entertainment looked as though it was going to be assimilated, like religion, to therapy. The arts could save themselves from this leveling down only by demonstrating that the kind of experience they provided was valuable in its own right and not to be obtained from any other kind of activity. [7]

Despite this defensive intellectual stance, the arts have nonetheless continued to gravitate, if not towards entertainment, then certainly towards commodity and—in the case of that which Charles Jencks has since classified as Post-Modern Architecture[8]—towards pure technique or pure scenography. In the latter case, the so-called postmodern architects are merely feeding the media-society with gratuitous, quietistic images rather than proffering, as they claim, a creative *rappel à l'ordre* after the supposedly proven bankruptcy of the liberative modern project. In this regard, as Andreas Huyssens has written, "The American postmodernist avant-garde, therefore, is not only the end game of avant-gardism. It also represents the fragmentation and decline of critical adversary culture." [9]

Nevertheless, it is true that modernization can no longer be simplistically identified as liberative *in se,* in part because of the domination of mass culture by the media-industry (above all television which, as Jerry Mander reminds us, expanded its persuasive power a thousandfold between 1945 and 1975[10]) and in part because the trajectory of modernization has brought us to the threshold of nuclear war and the annihilation of the entire species. So too, avant-gardism can no longer be sustained as a liberative moment, in part because its initial utopian promise has been overrun by the internal rationality of instrumental reason. This "closure" was perhaps best formulated by Herbert Marcuse when he wrote:

> The technological *apriori* is a political *apriori* inasmuch as the transformation of nature involves that of man, and inasmuch as the "man-made creations" issue from and re-enter the societal ensemble. One may still insist that the machinery of the technological universe is "as such" indifferent towards political ends—it can revolutionize or retard society. . . . However, when technics becomes the universal form of material production, it circumscribes an entire culture, it projects a historical totality—a "world." [11]

3. Critical Regionalism and World Culture

Architecture can only be sustained today as a critical practice if it assumes an *arrière-garde* position, that is to say, one which distances itself equally from the Enlightenment myth of progress and from a reactionary, unrealistic impulse to return to the architectonic forms of the preindustrial past. A critical arrière-garde has to remove itself from both the optimization of advanced technology and the ever-present tendency to regress into nostalgic historicism or the glibly decorative. It is my contention that only an arrière-garde has the capacity to cultivate a resistant, identity-giving culture while at the same time having discreet recourse to universal technique.

It is necessary to qualify the term arrière-garde so as to diminish its critical scope from such conservative policies as Populism or sentimental Regionalism with which it has often been associated. In order to ground arrière-gardism in a rooted yet critical strategy, it is helpful to appropriate the term Critical Regionalism as coined by Alex Tzonis and Liliane Lefaivre in "The Grid and the Pathway" (1981); in this essay they caution against the ambiguity of regional reformism, as this has become occasionally manifest since the last quarter of the 19th century:

> Regionalism has dominated architecture in almost all countries at some time during the past two centuries and a half. By way of general definition we can say that it upholds the individual and local architectonic features against more universal and abstract ones. In addition, however, regionalism bears the hallmark of ambiguity. On the one hand, it has been associated with movements of reform and liberation; . . . on the other, it has proved a powerful tool of repression and chauvinism. . . . Certainly, critical regionalism has its limitations. The upheaval of the populist movement—a more developed form of regionalism—has brought to light these weak points. No new architecture can emerge without a new kind of relations between designer and user, with-

out new kinds of programs. . . . Despite these limitations critical regionalism is a bridge over which any humanistic architecture of the future must pass.[12]

The fundamental strategy of Critical Regionalism is to mediate the impact of universal civilization with elements derived *indirectly* from the peculiarities of a particular place. It is clear from the above that Critical Regionalism depends upon maintaining a high level of critical self-consciousness. It may find its governing inspiration in such things as the range and quality of the local light, or in a *tectonic* derived from a peculiar structural mode, or in the topography of a given site.

But it is necessary, as I have already suggested, to distinguish between Critical Regionalism and simple-minded attempts to revive the hypothetical forms of a lost vernacular. In contradistinction to Critical Regionalism, the primary vehicle of Populism is the *communicative* or *instrumental* sign. Such a sign seeks to evoke not a critical perception of reality, but rather the sublimation of a desire for direct experience through the provision of information. Its tactical aim is to attain, as economically as possible, a preconceived level of gratification in behavioristic terms. In this respect, the strong affinity of Populism for the rhetorical techniques and imagery of advertising is hardly accidental. Unless one guards against such a convergence, one will confuse the resistant capacity of a critical practice with the demagogic tendencies of Populism.

The case can be made that Critical Regionalism as a cultural strategy is as much a bearer of *world culture* as it is a vehicle of *universal civilization*. And while it is obviously misleading to conceive of our inheriting world culture to the same degree as we are all heirs to universal civilization, it is nonetheless evident that since we are, in principle, subject to the impact of both, we have no choice but to take cognizance today of their interaction. In this regard the practice of Critical Regionalism is contingent upon a process of double mediation. In the first place, it has to "deconstruct" the overall spectrum of world culture which it inevitably inherits; in the second place, it has to achieve, through synthetic contradiction, a manifest critique of universal civilization. To deconstruct world culture is to remove oneself from that eclecticism of the *fin de siècle* which appropriated alien, exotic forms in order to revitalize the expressivity of an enervated society. (One thinks of the "form-force" aesthetics of Henri van de Velde or the "whiplash-Arabesques" of Victor Horta.) On the other hand, the mediation of universal technique involves imposing limits on the optimization of industrial and postindustrial technology. The future necessity for re-synthesizing principles and elements drawn from diverse origins and quite different ideological sets seems to be alluded to by Ricoeur when he writes:

> No one can say what will become of our civilization when it has really met different civilizations by means other than the shock of conquest and

domination. But we have to admit that this encounter has not yet taken place at the level of an authentic dialogue. That is why we are in a kind of lull or interregnum in which we can no longer practice the dogmatism of a single truth and in which we are not yet capable of conquering the skepticism into which we have stepped.[13]

A parallel and complementary sentiment was expressed by the Dutch architect Aldo Van Eyck who, quite coincidentally, wrote at the same time: "Western civilization habitually identifies itself with civilization as such on the pontifical assumption that what is not like it is a deviation, less advanced, primitive, or, at best, exotically interesting at a safe distance."[14]

That Critical Regionalism cannot be simply based on the autochthonous forms of a specific region alone was well put by the Californian architect Hamilton Harwell Harris when he wrote, now nearly thirty years ago:

Opposed to the Regionalism of Restriction is another type of regionalism, the Regionalism of Liberation. This is the manifestation of a region that is especially in tune with the emerging thought of the time. We call such a manifestation "regional" only because it has not yet emerged elsewhere. . . . A region may develop ideas. A region may accept ideas. Imagination and intelligence are necessary for both. In California in the late Twenties and Thirties modern European ideas met a still-developing regionalism. In New England, on the other hand, European Modernism met a rigid and restrictive regionalism that at first resisted and then surrendered. New England accepted European Modernism whole because its own regionalism had been reduced to a collection of restrictions.[15]

The scope for achieving a self-conscious synthesis between universal civilization and world culture may be specifically illustrated by Jørn Utzon's Bagsvaerd Church, built near Copenhagen in 1976, a work whose complex meaning stems directly from a revealed conjunction between, on the one hand, the *rationality* of normative technique and, on the other, the *arationality* of idiosyncratic form. Inasmuch as this building is organized around a regular grid and is comprised of repetitive, in-fill modules—concrete blocks in the first instance and precast concrete wall units in the second—we may justly regard it as the outcome of universal civilization. Such a building system, comprising an *in situ* concrete frame with prefabricated concrete in-fill elements, has indeed been applied countless times all over the developed world. However, the universality of this productive method—which includes, in this instance, patent glazing on the roof—is abruptly mediated when one passes from the optimal modular skin of the exterior to the far less optimal reinforced concrete shell vault spanning the nave. This last is obviously a relatively uneconomic mode of construction, selected and manipulated first for its direct associative capacity—that is to say, the vault signifies sacred space—and second for its

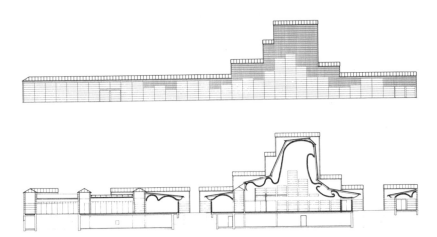

Jørn Utzon, *Bagsvaerd Church,* 1973-76.
North elevation and section.

multiple cross-cultural references. While the reinforced concrete shell vault
has long since held an established place within the received tectonic canon of
Western modern architecture, the highly configured section adopted in
this instance is hardly familiar, and the only precedent for such a form, in a
sacred context, is Eastern rather than Western—namely, the Chinese
pagoda roof, cited by Utzon in his seminal essay of 1963, "Platforms and
Plateaus." [16] Although the main Bagsvaerd vault spontaneously signifies
its religious nature, it does so in such a way as to preclude an exclusively
Occidental or Oriental reading of the code by which the public and sacred
space is constituted. The intent of this expression is, of course, to secularize
the sacred form by precluding the usual set of semantic religious references
and thereby the corresponding range of automatic responses that usually
accompany them. This is arguably a more appropriate way of rendering a
church in a highly secular age, where any symbolic allusion to the
ecclesiastic usually degenerates immediately into the vagaries of kitsch.
And yet paradoxically, this desacralization at Bagsvaerd subtly reconstitutes
a renewed basis for the spiritual, one founded, I would argue, in a regional
reaffirmation—grounds, at least, for some form of collective spirituality.

4. The Resistance of the Place-Form

The Megalopolis recognized as such in 1961 by the geographer Jean Gottman[17] continues to proliferate throughout the developed world to such an extent that, with the exception of cities which were laid in place before the turn of the century, we are no longer able to maintain defined urban forms. The last quarter of a century has seen the so-called field of urban design degenerate into a theoretical subject whose discourse bears little relation to the processal realities of modern development. Today even the super-managerial discipline of urban planning has entered into a state of crisis. The ultimate fate of the plan which was officially promulgated for the rebuilding of Rotterdam after World War II is symptomatic in this regard, since it testifies, in terms of its own recently changed status, to the current tendency to reduce all planning to little more than the allocation of land use and the logistics of distribution. Until relatively recently, the Rotterdam master plan was revised and upgraded every decade in the light of buildings which had been realized in the interim. In 1975, however, this progressive urban cultural procedure was unexpectedly abandoned in favor of publishing a nonphysical, infrastructure plan conceived at a regional scale. Such a plan concerns itself almost exclusively with the logistical projection of changes in land use and with the augmentation of existing distribution systems.

In his essay of 1954, "Building, Dwelling, Thinking," Martin Heidegger provides us with a critical vantage point from which to behold this phenomenon of universal placelessness. Against the Latin or, rather, the antique *abstract* concept of space as a more or less endless continuum of evenly subdivided spatial components or integers—what he terms *spatium* and *extensio*—Heidegger opposes the German word for space (or, rather, place), which is the term *Raum*. Heidegger argues that the phenomenological essence of such a space/place depends upon the *concrete,* clearly defined nature of its boundary, for, as he puts it, "A boundary is not that at which something stops, but, as the Greeks recognized, the boundary is that from which something begins its presencing." [18] Apart from confirming that Western abstract reason has its origins in the antique culture of the Mediterranean, Heidegger shows that etymologically the German gerund *building* is closely linked with the archaic forms of *being, cultivating* and *dwelling,* and goes on to state that the condition of "dwelling" and hence ultimately of "being" can only take place in a domain that is clearly bounded.

While we may well remain skeptical as to the merit of grounding critical practice in a concept so hermetically metaphysical as Being, we are, when confronted with the ubiquitous placelessness of our modern environment, nonetheless brought to posit, after Heidegger, the absolute precondition of a bounded domain in order to create an architecture of resistance. Only such a defined boundary will permit the built form to stand against—and hence literally to withstand in an institutional sense—the endless processal flux of the Megalopolis.

The bounded place-form, in its public mode, is also essential to what Hannah Arendt has termed "the space of human appearance," since the evolution of legitimate power has always been predicated upon the existence of the "polis" and upon comparable units of institutional and physical form. While the political life of the Greek polis did not stem directly from the physical presence and representation of the city-state, it displayed in contrast to the Megalopolis the cantonal attributes of urban density. Thus Arendt writes in *The Human Condition:*

> The only indispensable material factor in the generation of power is the living together of people. Only where men live so close together that the potentialities for action are always present will power remain with them and the foundation of cities, which as city states have remained paradigmatic for all Western political organization, is therefore the most important material prerequisite for power.[19]

Nothing could be more removed from the political essence of the city-state than the rationalizations of positivistic urban planners such as Melvin Webber, whose ideological concepts of *community without propinquity* and the *non-place urban realm* are nothing if not slogans devised to rationalize the absence of any true public realm in the modern motopia.[20] The manipulative bias of such ideologies has never been more openly expressed than in Robert Venturi's *Complexity and Contradiction in Architecture* (1966) wherein the author asserts that Americans do not need piazzas, since they should be at home watching television.[21] Such reactionary attitudes emphasize the impotence of an urbanized populace which has paradoxically lost the object of its urbanization.

While the strategy of Critical Regionalism as outlined above addresses itself mainly to the maintenance of an *expressive density and resonance* in an architecture of resistance (a cultural density which under today's conditions could be said to be potentially liberative in and of itself since it opens the user to manifold *experiences*), the provision of a place-form is equally essential to critical practice, inasmuch as a resistant architecture, in an institutional sense, is necessarily dependent on a clearly defined domain. Perhaps the most generic example of such an urban form is the perimeter block, although other related, introspective types may be evoked, such as the galleria, the atrium, the forecourt and the labyrinth. And while these types have in many instances today simply become the vehicles for accommodating psuedo-public realms (one thinks of recent megastructures in housing, hotels, shopping centers, etc.), one cannot even in these instances entirely discount the latent political and resistant potential of the place-form.

5. Culture Versus Nature: Topography, Context, Climate, Light and Tectonic Form

Critical Regionalism necessarily involves a more directly dialectical relation with nature than the more abstract, formal traditions of modern avant-garde architecture allow. It is self-evident that the *tabula rasa* tendency of modernization favors the optimum use of earth-moving equipment inasmuch as a totally flat datum is regarded as the most economic matrix upon which to predicate the rationalization of construction. Here again, one touches in concrete terms this fundamental opposition between universal civilization and autochthonous culture. The bulldozing of an irregular topography into a flat site is clearly a technocratic gesture which aspires to a condition of absolute *placelessness,* whereas the terracing of the same site to receive the stepped form of a building is an engagement in the act of "cultivating" the site.

Clearly such a mode of beholding and acting brings one close once again to Heidegger's etymology; at the same time, it evokes the method alluded to by the Swiss architect Mario Botta as "building the site." It is possible to argue that in this last instance the specific culture of the region—that is to say, its history in both a geological and agricultural sense—becomes inscribed into the form and realization of the work. This inscription, which arises out of "in-laying" the building into the site, has many levels of significance, for it has a capacity to embody, in built form, the prehistory of the place, its archeological past and its subsequent cultivation and transformation across time. Through this layering into the site the idiosyncrasies of place find their expression without falling into sentimentality.

What is evident in the case of topography applies to a similar degree in the case of an existing urban fabric, and the same can be claimed for the contingencies of climate and the temporally inflected qualities of local light. Once again, the sensitive modulation and incorporation of such factors must almost by definition be fundamentally opposed to the optimum use of universal technique. This is perhaps most clear in the case of light and climate control. The generic window is obviously the most delicate point at which these two natural forces impinge upon the outer membrane of the building, fenestration having an innate capacity to inscribe architecture with the character of a region and hence to express the place in which the work is situated.

Until recently, the received precepts of modern curatorial practice favored the exclusive use of artificial light in all art galleries. It has perhaps been insufficiently recognized how this encapsulation tends to reduce the artwork to a commodity, since such an environment must conspire to render the work placeless. This is because the local light spectrum is never permitted to play across its surface: here, then, we see how the loss of aura, attributed by Walter Benjamin to the processes of mechanical reproduction, also arises from a relatively static application of universal technology. The converse of this "placeless" practice would be to provide that art galleries be top-lit through carefully contrived monitors so that, while the injurious effects of direct sunlight are avoided, the ambient light of the exhibition volume changes under the impact of time, season, humidity, etc. Such conditions guarantee the appearance of a place-conscious poetic—a form of filtration compounded out of an interaction between culture and nature, between art and light. Clearly this principle applies to all fenestration, irrespective of size and location. A constant "regional inflection" of the form arises directly from the fact that in certain climates the glazed aperture is advanced, while in others it is recessed behind the masonry facade (or, alternatively, shielded by adjustable sun breakers).

The way in which such openings provide for appropriate ventilation also constitutes an unsentimental element reflecting the nature of local culture. Here, clearly, the main antagonist of rooted culture is the ubiquitous air-conditioner, applied in all times and in all places, irrespective of the local climatic conditions which have a capacity to express the specific place and the seasonal variations of its climate. Wherever they occur, the fixed window and the remote-controlled air-conditioning system are mutually indicative of domination by universal technique.

Despite the critical importance of topography and light, the primary principle of architectural autonomy resides in the *tectonic* rather than the *scenographic:* that is to say, this autonomy is embodied in the revealed ligaments of the construction and in the way in which the syntactical form of the structure explicitly resists the action of gravity. It is obvious that this discourse of the load borne (the beam) and the load-bearing (the column) cannot be brought into being where the structure is masked or otherwise concealed. On the other hand, the tectonic is not to be confused with the purely technical, for it is more than the simple revelation of stereotomy or the expression of skeletal framework. Its essence was first defined by the German aesthetician Karl Bötticher in his book *Die Tektonik der Hellenen* (1852); and it was perhaps best summarized by the architectural historian Stanford Anderson when he wrote:

> *"Tektonik"* referred not just to the activity of making the materially requisite construction . . . but rather to the activity that raises this construction to an art

form.... The functionally adequate form must be adapted so as to give expression to its function. The sense of bearing provided by the entasis of Greek columns became the touchstone of this concept of *Tektonik*.[22]

The tectonic remains to us today as a potential means for distilling play between material, craftwork and gravity, so as to yield a component which is in fact a condensation of the entire structure. We may speak here of the presentation of a structural poetic rather than the re-presentation of a facade.

6. The Visual Versus the Tactile

The tactile resilience of the place-form and the capacity of the body to read the environment in terms other than those of sight alone suggest a potential strategy for resisting the domination of universal technology. It is symptomatic of the priority given to sight that we find it necessary to remind ourselves that the tactile is an important dimension in the perception of built form. One has in mind a whole range of complementary sensory perceptions which are registered by the labile body: the intensity of light, darkness, heat and cold; the feeling of humidity; the aroma of material; the almost palpable presence of masonry as the body senses its own confinement; the momentum of an induced gait and the relative inertia of the body as it traverses the floor; the echoing resonance of our own footfall. Luchino Visconti was well aware of these factors when making the film *The Damned,* for he insisted that the main set of the Altona mansion should be paved in real wooden parquet. It was his belief that without a solid floor underfoot the actors would be incapable of assuming appropriate and convincing postures.

A similar tactile sensitivity is evident in the finishing of the public circulation in Alvar Aalto's Säynatsalo Town Hall of 1952. The main route leading to the second-floor council chamber is ultimately orchestrated in terms which are as much tactile as they are visual. Not only is the principal access stair lined in raked brickwork, but the treads and risers are also finished in brick. The kinetic impetus of the body in climbing the stair is thus checked by the friction of the steps, which are "read" soon after in contrast to the timber floor of the council chamber itself. This chamber asserts its honorific status through sound, smell and texture, not to mention the springy deflection of the floor underfoot (and a noticeable tendency to lose one's balance on its polished surface). From this example it is clear that the liberative importance of the tactile resides in the fact that it can only be decoded in terms of *experience* itself: it cannot be reduced to mere information, to representation or to the simple evocation of a simulacrum substituting for absent presences.

Alvar Aalto, *Säynatsalo Town Hall,* 1952.

In this way, Critical Regionalism seeks to complement our normative visual experience by readdressing the tactile range of human perceptions. In so doing, it endeavors to balance the priority accorded to the image and to counter the Western tendency to interpret the environment in exclusively perspectival terms. According to its etymology, perspective means rationalized sight or clear seeing, and as such it presupposes a conscious suppression of the senses of smell, hearing and taste, and a consequent distancing from a more direct experience of the environment. This self-imposed limitation relates to that which Heidegger has called a "loss of nearness." In attempting to counter this loss, the tactile opposes itself to the scenographic and the drawing of veils over the surface of reality. Its capacity to arouse the impulse to touch returns the architect to the poetics of construction and to the erection of works in which the tectonic value of each component depends upon the density of its objecthood. The tactile and the tectonic jointly have the capacity to transcend the mere appearance of the technical in much the same way as the place-form has the potential to withstand the relentless onslaught of global modernization.

References

1. Paul Ricoeur, "Universal Civilization and National Cultures" (1961), *History and Truth,* trans. Chas. A. Kelbley (Evanston: Northwestern University Press, 1965), pp. 276-7.
2. That these are but two sides of the same coin has perhaps been most dramatically demonstrated in the Portland City Annex completed in Portland, Oregon in 1982 to the designs of Michael Graves. The constructional fabric of this building bears no relation whatsoever to the "representative" scenography that is applied to the building both inside and out.
3. Ricoeur, p. 277.
4. Fernand Braudel informs us that the term "culture" hardly existed before the beginning of the 19th century when, as far as Anglo-Saxon letters are concerned, it already finds itself opposed to "civilization" in the writings of Samuel Taylor Coleridge—above all, in Coleridge's *On the Constitution of Church and State* of 1830. The noun "civilization" has a somewhat longer history, first appearing in 1766, although its verb and participle forms date to the 16th and 17th centuries. The use that Ricoeur makes of the opposition between these two terms relates to the work of 20th-century German thinkers and writers such as Osvald Spengler, Ferdinand Tönnies, Alfred Weber and Thomas Mann.
5. Hannah Arendt, *The Human Condition* (Chicago: University of Chicago Press, 1958), p. 154.
6. Clement Greenberg, "Avant-Garde and Kitsch," in Gillo Dorfles, ed., *Kitsch* (New York: Universe Books, 1969), p. 126.
7. Greenberg, "Modernist Painting," in Gregory Battcock, ed., *The New Art* (New York: Dutton, 1966), pp. 101-2.
8. See Charles Jencks, *The Language of Post-Modern Architecture* (New York: Rizzoli, 1977).
9. Andreas Huyssens, "The Search for Tradition: Avant-Garde and Postmodernism in the 1970s," *New German Critique,* 22 (Winter 1981), p. 34.
10. Jerry Mander, *Four Arguments for the Elimination of Television* (New York: Morrow Quill, 1978), p. 134.
11. Herbert Marcuse, *One-Dimensional Man* (Boston: Beacon Press, 1964), p. 156.
12. Alex Tzonis and Liliane Lefaivre, "The Grid and the Pathway. An Introduction to the Work of Dimitris and Susana Antonakakis," *Architecture in Greece,* 15 (Athens: 1981), p. 178.
13. Ricoeur, p. 283.
14. Aldo Van Eyck, *Forum* (Amsterdam: 1962).
15. Hamilton Harwell Harris, "Liberative and Restrictive Regionalism." Address given to the Northwest Chapter of the AIA in Eugene, Oregon in 1954.
16. Jørn Utzon, "Platforms and Plateaus: Ideas of a Danish Architect," *Zodiac,* 10 (Milan: Edizioni Communita, 1963), pp. 112-14.
17. Jean Gottmann, *Megalopolis* (Cambridge: MIT Press, 1961).
18. Martin Heidegger, "Building, Dwelling, Thinking," in *Poetry, Language, Thought* (New York: Harper Colophon, 1971), p. 154. This essay first appeared in German in 1954.
19. Arendt, p. 201.
20. Melvin Webber, *Explorations in Urban Structure* (Philadelphia: University of Pennsylvania Press, 1964).
21. Robert Venturi, *Complexity and Contradiction in Architecture* (New York: Museum of Modern Art, 1966), p. 133.
22. Stanford Anderson, "Modern Architecture and Industry: Peter Behrens, the AEG, and Industrial Design," *Oppositions* 21 (Summer 1980), p. 83.

Sculpture in the Expanded Field

ROSALIND KRAUSS

Toward the center of the field there is a slight mound, a swelling in the earth, which is the only warning given for the presence of the work. Closer to it, the large square face of the pit can be seen, as can the ends of the ladder that is needed to descend into the excavation. The work itself is thus entirely below grade: half atrium, half tunnel, the boundary between outside and in, a delicate structure of wooden posts and beams. The work, *Perimeters/ Pavilions/Decoys*, 1978, by Mary Miss, is of course a sculpture or, more precisely, an earthwork.

Over the last ten years rather surprising things have come to be called sculpture: narrow corridors with TV monitors at the ends; large photographs documenting country hikes; mirrors placed at strange angles in ordinary rooms; temporary lines cut into the floor of the desert. Nothing, it would seem, could possibly give to such a motley of effort the right to lay claim to whatever one might mean by the category of sculpture. Unless, that is, the category can be made to become almost infinitely malleable.

The critical operations that have accompanied postwar American art have largely worked in the service of this manipulation. In the hands of this criticism categories like sculpture and painting have been kneaded and stretched and twisted in an extraordinary demonstration of elasticity, a display of the way a cultural term can be extended to include just about anything. And though this pulling and stretching of a term such as sculpture is overtly performed in the name of vanguard aesthetics—the ideology of the new—its covert message is that of historicism. The new is made comfortable by being made familiar, since it is seen as having gradually evolved from the forms of the past. Historicism works on the new and different to diminish newness and mitigate difference. It makes a place for

This essay was originally published in *October* 8 (Spring, 1979) and is reprinted here by permission of the author.

Mary Miss: *Perimeters/Pavillions/Decoys,* 1978.
Nassau County, Long Island, New York.

change in our experience by evoking the model of evolution, so that the man
who now is can be accepted as being different from the child he once was,
by simultaneously being seen—through the unseeable action of the telos—
as the same. And we are comforted by this perception of sameness, this
strategy for reducing anything foreign in either time or space, to what we
already know and are.

No sooner had minimal sculpture appeared on the horizon of the aesthetic
experience of the 1960s than criticism began to construct a paternity for this
work, a set of constructivist fathers who could legitimize and thereby
authenticate the strangeness of these objects. Plastic? inert geometries?
factory production?—none of this was *really* strange, as the ghosts of Gabo
and Tatlin and Lissitzky could be called in to testify. Never mind that the
content of the one had nothing to do with, was in fact the exact opposite of,
the content of the other. Never mind that Gabo's celluloid was the sign of
lucidity and intellection, while Judd's plastic-tinged-with-dayglo spoke the
hip patois of California. It did not matter that constructivist forms were

intended as visual proof of the immutable logic and coherence of universal geometries, while their seeming counterparts in minimalism were demonstrably contingent—denoting a universe held together not by Mind but by guy wires, or glue, or the accidents of gravity. The rage to historicize simply swept these differences aside.

Of course, with the passing of time these sweeping operations got a little harder to perform. As the 1960s began to lengthen into the 1970s and "sculpture" began to be piles of thread waste on the floor, or sawed redwood timbers rolled into the gallery, or tons of earth excavated from the desert, or stockades of logs surrounded by firepits the word *sculpture* became harder to pronounce—but not really that much harder. The historian/critic simply performed a more extended sleight-of-hand and began to construct his genealogies out of the data of millenia rather than decades. Stonehenge, the Nazca lines, the Toltec ballcourts, Indian burial mounds—anything at all could be hauled into court to bear witness to this work's connection to history and thereby to legitimize its status as sculpture. Of course Stonehenge and the Toltec ballcourts were just exactly *not* sculpture, and so their role as historicist precedent becomes somewhat suspect in this particular demonstration. But never mind. The trick can still be done by calling upon a variety of primitivizing work from the earlier part of the century—Brancusi's *Endless Column* will do—to mediate between extreme past and present.

But in doing all of this, the very term we had thought we were saving— *sculpture*—has begun to be somewhat obscured. We had thought to use a universal category to authenticate a group of particulars, but the category has now been forced to cover such a heterogeneity that it is, itself, in danger of collapsing. And so we stare at the pit in the earth and think we both do and don't know what sculpture is.

Yet I would submit that we know very well what sculpture is. And one of the things we know is that it is a historically bounded category and not a universal one. As is true of any other convention, sculpture has its own internal logic, its own set of rules, which, though they can be applied to a variety of situations, are not themselves open to very much change. The logic of sculpture, it would seem, is inseparable from the logic of the monument. By virtue of this logic a sculpture is a commemorative representation. It sits in a particular place and speaks in a symbolical tongue about the meaning or use of that place. The equestrian statue of Marcus Aurelius is such a monument, set in the center of the Campidoglio to represent by its symbolical presence the relationship between ancient, Imperial Rome and the seat of government of modern, Renaissance Rome. Bernini's statue of the *Conversion of Constantine,* placed at the foot of the Vatican stairway connecting the Basilica of St. Peter to the heart of the papacy is another such monument, a marker at a particular place for a specific meaning/event.

Auguste Rodin: *Balzac*, 1897.

Because they thus function in relation to the logic of representation and marking, sculptures are normally figurative and vertical, their pedestals an important part of the sculpture since they mediate between actual site and representational sign. There is nothing very mysterious about this logic; understood and inhabited, it was the source of a tremendous production of sculpture during centuries of Western art.

But the convention is not immutable and there came a time when the logic began to fail. Late in the 19th century we witnessed the fading of the logic of the monument. It happened rather gradually. But two cases come to mind, both bearing the marks of their own transitional status. Rodin's *Gates of Hell* and his statue of *Balzac* were both conceived as monuments. The first were commissioned in 1880 as the doors to a projected museum of decorative arts; the second was commissioned in 1891 as a memorial to literary genius to be set up at a specific site in Paris. The failure of these two works as monuments is signaled not only by the fact that multiple versions can be found in a variety of museums in various countries, while no version exists on the original sites — both commissions having eventually collapsed. Their failure is also encoded onto the very surfaces of these works: the doors having been gouged away and anti-structurally encrusted to the point where they bear their inoperative condition on their face; the *Balzac* executed with such a degree of subjectivity that not even Rodin believed (as letters by him attest) that the work would ever be accepted.

With these two sculptural projects, I would say, one crosses the threshold of the logic of the monument, entering the space of what could be called its negative condition — a kind of sitelessness, or homelessness, an absolute loss of place. Which is to say one enters modernism, since it is the modernist period of sculptural production that operates in relation to this loss of site, producing the monument as abstraction, the monument as pure marker or base, functionally placeless and largely self-referential.

It is these two characteristics of modernist sculpture that declare its status, and therefore its meaning and function, as essentially nomadic. Through its fetishization of the base, the sculpture reaches downward to absorb the pedestal into itself and away from actual place; and through the representation of its own materials or the process of its construction, the sculpture depicts its own autonomy. Brancusi's art is an extraordinary instance of the way this happens. The base becomes, in a work like the *Cock,* the morphological generator of the figurative part of the object; in the *Caryatids* and *Endless Column,* the sculpture is all base; while in *Adam and Eve,* the sculpture is in a reciprocal relation to its base. The base is thus defined as essentially transportable, the marker of the work's homelessness integrated into the very fiber of the sculpture. And Brancusi's interest in expressing parts of the body as fragments that tend toward radical abstractness also testifies to a loss of site, in this case the site of the rest of the body, the skeletal support that would give to one of the bronze or marble heads a home.

In being the negative condition of the monument, modernist sculpture had a kind of idealist space to explore, a domain cut off from the project of temporal and spatial representation, a vein that was rich and new and could for a while be profitably mined. But it was a limited vein and, having been opened in the early part of the century, it began by about 1950 to be exhausted. It began, that is, to be experienced more and more as pure negativity. At this point modernist sculpture appeared as a kind of black hole in the space of consciousness, something whose positive content was increasingly difficult to define, something that was possible to locate only in terms of what it was not. "Sculpture is what you bump into when you back up to see a painting," Barnett Newman said in the '50s. But it would probably be more accurate to say of the work that one found in the early '60s that sculpture had entered a categorical no-man's-land: it was what was on or in front of a building that was not a building, or what was in the landscape that was not the landscape.

The purest examples that come to mind from the early 1960s are both by Robert Morris. One is the work exhibited in 1964 in the Green Gallery— quasi-architectural integers whose status as sculpture reduces almost completely to the simple determination that it is what is in the room that is not really the room; the other is the outdoor exhibition of the mirrored boxes—forms which are distinct from the setting only because, though visually continuous with grass and trees, they are not in fact part of the landscape.

In this sense sculpture had entered the full condition of its inverse logic and had become pure negativity: the combination of exclusions. Sculpture, it could be said, had ceased being a positivity, and was now the category that resulted from the addition of the *not-landscape* to the *not-architecture*. Diagrammatically expressed, the limit of modernist sculpture, the addition of the neither/nor, looks like this:

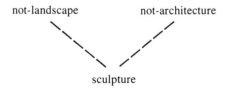

Now, if sculpture itself had become a kind of ontological absence, the combination of exclusions, the sum of the neither/nor, that does not mean that the terms themselves from which it was built—the *not-landscape* and the *not-architecture*—did not have a certain interest. This is because these terms express a strict opposition between the built and the not-built, the cultural and the natural, between which the production of sculptural art appeared to be suspended. And what began to happen in the career of one sculptor after another, beginning at the end of the 1960s, is that attention began to focus on the outer limits of those terms of exclusion. For, if those terms are the expression of a logical opposition stated as a pair of negatives, they can be transformed by a simple inversion into the same polar opposites but expressed positively. That is, the *not-architecture* is, according to the logic of a certain kind of expansion, just another way of expressing the term *landscape,* and the *not-landscape* is, simply, *architecture.* The expansion to which I am referring is called a Klein group when employed mathematically and has various other designations, among them the Piaget group, when used by structuralists involved in mapping operations within the human sciences. By means of this logical expansion a set of binaries is transformed into a quaternary field which both mirrors the original opposition and at the same time opens it. It becomes a logically expanded field which looks like this:

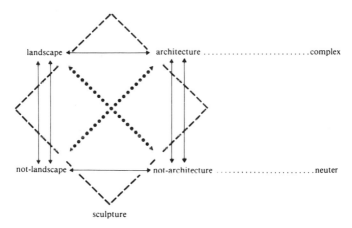

The dimensions of this structure may be analyzed as follows: 1) there are two relationships of pure contradiction which are termed *axes* (and further differentiated into the *complex axis* and the *neuter axis*) and are designated by the solid arrows (see diagram); 2) there are two relationships of contradiction, expressed as involution, which are called *schemas* and are designated by the double arrows; and 3) there are two relationships of implication which are called *deixes* and are designated by the broken arrows.[1]

Another way of saying this is that even though *sculpture* may be reduced to what is in the Klein group the neuter term of the *not-landscape* plus the *not-architecture,* there is no reason not to imagine an opposite term—one that would be both *landscape* and *architecture*—which within this schema is called the *complex*. But to think the complex is to admit into the realm of art two terms that had formerly been prohibited from it: *landscape* and *architecture* — terms that could function to define the sculptural (as they had begun to do in modernism) only in their negative or neuter condition. Because it was ideologically prohibited, the complex had remained excluded from what might be called the closure of post-Renaissance art. Our culture had not before been able to think the complex, although other cultures have thought this term with great ease. Labyrinths and mazes are *both* landscape and architecture; Japanese gardens are *both* landscape and architecture; the ritual playing fields and processionals of ancient civilizations were all in this sense the unquestioned occupants of the complex. Which is *not* to say that they were an early, or a degenerate, or a variant form of sculpture. They were part of a universe or cultural space in which sculpture was simply another part — not somehow, as our historicist minds would have it, the same. Their purpose and pleasure is exactly that they are opposite and different.

The expanded field is thus generated by problematizing the set of oppositions between which the modernist category *sculpture* is suspended. And once this has happened, once one is able to think one's way into this expansion, there are — logically — three other categories that one can envision, all of them a condition of the field itself, and none of them assimilable to *sculpture*. Because as we can see, *sculpture* is no longer the privileged middle term between two things that it isn't. *Sculpture* is rather only one term on the periphery of a field in which there are other, differently structured possibilities. And one has thereby gained the "permission" to think these other forms. So our diagram is filled in as follows:

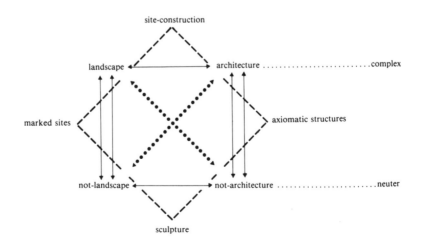

Alice Aycock: *Maze*, 1972.

It seems fairly clear that this permission (or pressure) to think the expanded field was felt by a number of artists at about the same time, roughly between the years 1968 and 1970. For one after another Robert Morris, Robert Smithson, Michael Heizer, Richard Serra, Walter De Maria, Robert Irwin, Sol LeWitt, Bruce Nauman... had entered a situation the logical conditions of which can no longer be described as modernist. In order to name this historical rupture and the structural transformation of the cultural field that characterizes it, one must have recourse to another term. The one already in use in other areas of criticism is postmodernism. There seems no reason not to use it.

But whatever term one uses, the evidence is already in. By 1970, with the *Partially Buried Woodshed* at Kent State University, in Ohio, Robert Smithson had begun to occupy the complex axis, which for ease of reference I am calling *site construction*. In 1971 with the observatory he built in wood and sod in Holland, Robert Morris had joined him. Since that time, many other artists—Robert Irwin, Alice Aycock, John Mason, Michael Heizer, Mary Miss, Charles Simonds—have operated within this new set of possibilities.

Robert Smithson: *First Mirror Displacement,* Yucatan, 1969.

Similarly, the possible combination of *landscape* and *not-landscape* began to be explored in the late 1960s. The term *marked sites* is used to identify work like Smithson's *Spiral Jetty* (1970) and Heizer's *Double Negative* (1969), as it also describes some of the work in the '70s by Serra, Morris, Carl Andre, Dennis Oppenheim, Nancy Holt, George Trakis, and many others. But in addition to actual physical manipulations of sites, this term also refers to other forms of marking. These might operate through the application of impermanent marks—Heizer's *Depressions,* Oppenheim's *Time Lines,* or De Maria's *Mile Long Drawing,* for example—or through the use of photography. Smithson's *Mirror Displacements in the Yucatan* were probably the first widely known instances of this, but since then the work of Richard Long and Hamish Fulton has focused on the photographic experience of marking. Christo's *Running Fence* might be said to be an impermanent, photographic, and political instance of marking a site.

The first artists to explore the possibilities of *architecture* plus *not-architecture* were Robert Irwin, Sol LeWitt, Bruce Nauman, Richard Serra, and Christo. In every case of these *axiomatic structures,* there is some kind of intervention into the real space of architecture, sometimes through partial reconstruction, sometimes through drawing, or as in the recent works of Morris, through the use of mirrors. As was true of the category of the *marked site,* photography can be used for this purpose; I am thinking here of the video corridors by Nauman. But whatever the medium employed, the possibility explored in this category is a process of mapping the axiomatic features of the architectural experience—the abstract conditions of openness and closure—onto the reality of a given space.

The expanded field which characterizes this domain of postmodernism possesses two features that are already implicit in the above description. One of these concerns the practice of individual artists; the other has to do with the question of medium. At both these points the bounded conditions of modernism have suffered a logically determined rupture.

With regard to individual practice, it is easy to see that many of the artists in question have found themselves occupying, successively, different places within the expanded field. And though the experience of the field suggests that this continual relocation of one's energies is entirely logical, an art criticism still in the thrall of a modernist ethos has been largely suspicious of such movement, calling it eclectic. This suspicion of a career that moves continually and erratically beyond the domain of sculpture obviously derives from the modernist demand for the purity and separateness of the various mediums (and thus the necessary specialization of a practitioner within a given medium). But what appears as eclectic from one point of view can be seen as rigorously logical from another. For, within the situation of postmodernism, practice is not defined in relation to a given medium—sculpture—but rather in relation to the logical operations on a set of cultural terms, for which any medium—photography, books, lines on walls, mirrors, or sculpture itself—might be used.

Thus the field provides both for an expanded but finite set of related positions for a given artist to occupy and explore, and for an organization of work that is not dictated by the conditions of a particular medium. From the structure laid out above, it is obvious that the logic of the space of postmodernist practice is no longer organized around the definition of a given medium on the grounds of material, or, for that matter, the perception of material. It is organized instead through the universe of terms that are felt to be in opposition within a cultural situation. (The postmodernist space of painting would obviously involve a similar expansion around a different set of terms from the pair *architecture/landscape*—a set that would probably turn on the opposition *uniqueness/reproducibility.*) It follows, then, that within any one of the positions generated by the given logical space, many different mediums might be employed. It follows as well that any single artist might occupy, successively, any one of the positions. And it also seems the case that within the limited position of sculpture itself the organization and content of much of the strongest work will reflect the condition of the logical space. I am thinking here of the sculpture of Joel Shapiro, which, though it positions itself in the neuter term, is involved in the setting of images of architecture within relatively vast fields (landscapes) of space. (These considerations apply, obviously, to other work as well— Charles Simonds, for example, or Ann and Patrick Poirier.)

I have been insisting that the expanded field of postmodernism occurs at a specific moment in the recent history of art. It is a historical event with a determinant structure. It seems to me extremely important to map that structure and that is what I have begun to do here. But clearly, since this is a matter of history, it is also important to explore a deeper set of questions which pertain to something more than mapping and involve instead the problem of explanation. These address the root cause—the conditions of possibility—that brought about the shift into postmodernism, as they also address the cultural determinants of the opposition through which a given field is structured. This is obviously a different approach to thinking about the history of form from that of historicist criticism's constructions of elaborate genealogical trees. It presupposes the acceptance of definitive ruptures and the possibility of looking at historical process from the point of view of logical structure.

Reference

1. For a discussion of the Klein group, see Marc Barbut, "On the Meaning of the Word 'Structure' in Mathematics," in Michael Lane, ed., *Introduction to Structuralism,* (New York, Basic Books, 1970); for an application of the Piaget group, see A.-J. Greimas and F. Rastier, "The Interaction of Semiotic Constraints," *Yale French Studies,* no. 41 (1968), 86-105.

On the Museum's Ruins

DOUGLAS CRIMP

The German word museal [*museumlike*] *has unpleasant overtones. It describes objects to which the observer no longer has a vital relationship and which are in the process of dying. They owe their preservation more to historical respect than to the needs of the present. Museum and mausoleum are connected by more than phonetic association. Museums are the family sepulchres of works of art.*
—Theodor W. Adorno, "Valéry Proust Museum"

In his review of the new installation of 19th-century art in the André Meyer Galleries of the Metropolitan Museum, Hilton Kramer attacked the inclusion of salon painting. Characterizing that art as silly, sentimental and impotent, Kramer went on to assert that, had the reinstallation been done a generation earlier, such pictures would have remained in the museum's storerooms to which they had so justly been consigned:

> It is the destiny of corpses, after all, to remain buried, and salon painting was found to be very dead indeed.
> But nowadays there is no art so dead that an art historian cannot be found to detect some simulacrum of life in its moldering remains. In the last decade, there has, in fact, arisen in the scholarly world a powerful sub-profession that specializes in these lugubrious disinterments.[1]

Kramer's metaphor of death and decay in the museum recalls Adorno's essay, in which the opposite but complementary experiences of Valéry and Proust at the Louvre are analyzed, except that Adorno insists upon this *museal* mortality as a necessary effect of an institution caught in the contradictions of its culture and therefore extending to every object contained there.[2] Kramer, on the other hand, retaining his faith in the eternal life of masterpieces, ascribes the conditions of life and death not to the museum or

This is a revised version of an essay that appeared in *October* 13 (Summer, 1980).

the particular history of which it is an instrument but to artworks themselves, their autonomous quality threatened only by the distortions that a particular misguided installation might impose. He therefore wishes to explain "this curious turnabout that places a meretricious little picture like Gérôme's *Pygmalion and Galatea* under the same roof with masterpieces on the order of Goya's *Pepito* and Manet's *Woman with a Parrot*. What kind of taste is it—or what standard of values—that can so easily accommodate such glaring opposites?"

> The answer [Kramer thinks] is to be found in that much-discussed phenomenon—the death of modernism. So long as the modernist movement was understood to be thriving, there could be no question about the revival of painters like Gérôme or Bouguereau. Modernism exerted a moral as well as an esthetic authority that precluded such a development. But the demise of modernism has left us with few, if any, defenses against the incursions of debased taste. Under the new post-modernist dispensation, anything goes. . . .
>
> It is an expression of this post-modernist ethos . . . that the new installation of 19th-century art at the Met needs . . . to be understood. What we are given in the beautiful André Meyer Galleries is the first comprehensive account of the 19th century from a post-modernist point of view in one of our major museums.[3]

We have here yet another example of Kramer's moralizing cultural conservatism disguised as progressive modernism. But we also have an interesting estimation of the discursive practice of the museum in the period of modernism and of its present transformation. Kramer's analysis fails, however, to take into account the extent to which the museum's claims to represent art coherently have already been opened to question by the practices of contemporary—postmodernist—art.

One of the first applications of the term *postmodernism* to the visual arts occurs in Leo Steinberg's "Other Criteria" in the course of a discussion of Robert Rauschenberg's transformation of the picture surface into what Steinberg calls a "flatbed," referring, significantly, to a printing press.[4] This flatbed picture plane is an altogether new kind of picture surface, one that effects, according to Steinberg, "the most radical shift in the subject matter of art, the shift from nature to culture." [5] That is to say, the flatbed is a surface which can receive a vast and heterogeneous array of cultural images and artifacts that had not been compatible with the pictorial field of either premodernist or modernist painting. (A modernist painting, in Steinberg's view, retains a "natural" orientation to the spectator's vision, which the postmodernist picture abandons.) Although Steinberg, writing in 1968, could not have had a very precise notion of the far-reaching implications of his term *postmodernism,* his reading of the revolution implicit in Rauschenberg's art can be both focused and extended by taking this designation seriously.

Presumably unintentionally, Steinberg's essay suggests important parallels with the "archeological" enterprise of Michel Foucault. Not only does the very term *postmodernism* imply the foreclosure of what Foucault would call the *èpistème*, or archive, of modernism, but even more specifically, by insisting upon the radically different kinds of picture surfaces upon which different kinds of data can be accumulated and organized, Steinberg selects the very figure that Foucault employs to represent the incompatibility of historical periods: the tables upon which their knowledge is tabulated. Foucault's project involves the replacement of those unities of humanist historical thought such as tradition, influence, development, evolution, source and origin with concepts like discontinuity, rupture, threshold, limit and transformation. Thus, in Foucault's terms, if the surface of a Rauschenberg painting truly involves the kind of transformation Steinberg claims it does, then it cannot be said to evolve from, or in any way be continuous with a modernist picture surface.[6] And if Rauschenberg's flatbed pictures are experienced as effecting such a rupture or discontinuity with the modernist past, as I believe they do and as I think do the works of many other artists of the present, then perhaps we are indeed experiencing one of those transformations in the epistemological field that Foucault describes. But it is not, of course, only the organization of knowledge that is unrecognizably transformed at certain moments in history. New institutions of power as well as new discourses arise; indeed, the two are interdependent. Foucault has analyzed the modern institutions of confinement—the asylum, the clinic and the prison—and their respective discursive formations—madness, illness and criminality. There is another such institution of confinement ripe for analysis in Foucault's terms—the museum—and another discipline—art history. They are the preconditions for the discourse that we know as modern art. And Foucault himself has suggested the way to begin thinking about this analysis.

The beginning of modernism in painting is usually located in Manet's work of the early 1860s, in which painting's relationship to its art-historical precedents was made shamelessly obvious. Titian's *Venus of Urbino* is meant to be as recognizable a vehicle for the picture of a modern courtesan in Manet's *Olympia* as is the unmodeled pink paint that composes her body. Just one hundred years after Manet thus rendered painting's relationship to its sources self-consciously problematic,[7] Rauschenberg made a series of pictures using images of Velázquez's *Rokeby Venus* and Ruben's *Venus at Her Toilet*. But Rauschenberg's references to these old-master paintings are effected entirely differently from Manet's; while Manet duplicates the pose, composition and certain details of the original in a painted transformation, Rauschenberg simply silkscreens a photographic reproduction of the

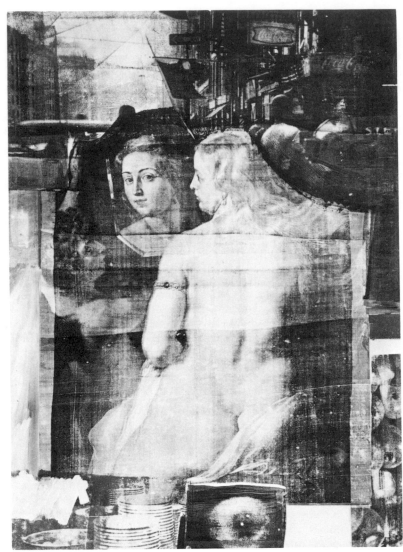

Robert Rauschenberg: *Persimmon,* 1964.

original onto a surface that might also contain such images as trucks and helicopters. And if trucks and helicopters cannot have found their way onto the surface of *Olympia,* it is obviously not only because such products of the modern age had not yet been invented; it is because of the structural coherence that made an image-bearing surface legible as a picture at the threshold of modernism, as opposed to the radically different pictorial logic that obtains at the beginning of postmodernism. Just what it is that constitutes the particular logic of a Manet painting is discussed by Foucault in an essay about Flaubert's *Temptation of St. Anthony:*

> *Déjeuner sur l'Herbe* and *Olympia* were perhaps the first "museum" paintings, the first paintings in European art that were less a response to the achievement of Giorgione, Raphael, and Velázquez than an acknowledgement (supported by this singular and obvious connection, using this legible reference to cloak its operation) of the new and substantial relationship of painting to itself, as a manifestation of the existence of museums and the particular reality and interdependence that paintings acquire in museums. In the same period, *The Temptation* was the first literary work to comprehend the greenish institutions where books are accumulated and where the slow and incontrovertible vegetation of learning quietly proliferates. Flaubert is to the library what Manet is to the museum. They both produced works in a self-conscious relationship to earlier paintings or texts — or rather to the aspect in painting or writing that remains indefinitely open. They erect their art within the archive. They were not meant to foster the lamentations — the lost youth, the absence of vigor, and the decline of inventiveness — through which we reproach our Alexandrian age, but to unearth an essential aspect of our culture: every painting now belongs within the squared and massive surface of painting and all literary works are confined to the indefinite murmur of writing.[8]

At a later point in this essay, Foucault says that *"Saint Anthony* seems to summon *Bouvard and Pécuchet,* at least to the extent that the latter stands as its grotesque shadow." If *The Temptation* points to the library as the generator of modern literature, then *Bouvard and Pécuchet* fingers it as the dumping grounds of an irredeemable classical culture. *Bouvard and Pécuchet* is a novel that systematically parodies the inconsistencies, irrelevancies, the massive foolishness of received ideas in the mid-19th century. Indeed, a "Dictionary of Received Ideas" was to comprise part of a second volume of Flaubert's last, unfinished novel.

Bouvard and Pécuchet is the narrative of two loony Parisian bachelors who, at a chance meeting, discover between themselves a profound sympathy, and also that they are both copy clerks. They share a distaste for city life and particularly for their fate of sitting behind desks all day. When Bouvard inherits a small fortune the two buy a farm in Normandy, to which they retire, expecting there to meet head-on the reality that was denied them in the half-life of their Parisian offices. They begin with the notion that they will farm their farm, at which they fail miserably. From agriculture they move to a more specialized field: arboriculture. Failing that they decide upon garden architecture. To prepare themselves for each of their new professions, they consult various manuals and treatises, in which they are extremely perplexed to find contradictions and misinformation of all kinds. The advice they find in them is either confusing or utterly inapplicable; theory and practice never coincide. But undaunted by their successive failures, they move on inexorably to the next activity, only to find that it too is incommensurate with the texts which purport to represent it. They try chemistry, physiology, anatomy, geology, archeology... the list goes on. When they finally succumb to the fact that the knowledge they've relied upon is a mass of contradictions, utterly haphazard and quite disjunct from the reality they'd sought to confront, they revert to their initial task of copying. Here is one of Flaubert's scenarios for the end of the novel:

> They copy papers haphazardly, everything they find, tobacco pouches, old newspapers, posters, torn books, etc. (real items and their imitations. Typical of each category).
> Then, they feel the need for a taxonomy. They make tables, antithetical oppositions such as "crimes of the kings and crimes of the people"—blessings of religion, crimes of religion. Beauties of history, etc.; sometimes, however, they have real problems putting each thing in its proper place and suffer great anxieties about it.
> —Onward! Enough speculation! Keep on copying! The page must be filled. Everything is equal, the good and the evil. The farcical and the sublime—the beautiful and the ugly—the insignificant and the typical, they all become an exaltation of the statistical. There are nothing but facts—and phenomena.
> Final bliss.[9]

In an essay about the novel, Eugenio Donato argues persuasively that the emblem for the series of heterogeneous activities of Bouvard and Pécuchet is not, as Foucault and others have claimed, the library-encyclopedia, but rather the museum. This is not only because the museum is a privileged term in the novel itself, but also because of the absolute heterogeneity it gathers together. The museum contains everything the library contains and it contains the library as well:

> If Bouvard and Pécuchet never assemble what can amount to a library, they nevertheless manage to constitute for themselves a private museum. The museum, in fact, occupies a central position in the novel; it is connected to the characters' interest in archeology, geology, and history and it is thus through the *Museum* that questions of origin, causality, representation, and symbolization are most clearly stated. The *Museum,* as well as the questions it tries to answer, depends upon an archeological epistemology. Its representational and

historical pretensions are based upon a number of metaphysical assumptions about origins—archeology intends, after all, to be a science of the *archēs*. Archeological origins are important in two ways: each archeological artifact has to be an original artifact, and these original artifacts must in turn explain the "meaning" of a subsequent larger history. Thus, in Flaubert's caricatural example, the baptismal font that Bouvard and Pécuchet discover has to be a Celtic sacrificial stone, and Celtic culture has in turn to act as an original master pattern for cultural history.[10]

Not only do Bouvard and Pécuchet derive all of Western culture from the few stones that remain from the Celtic past, but the "meaning" of that culture as well. Those menhirs lead them to construct the phallic wing of their museum:

> In former times, towers, pyramids, candles, milestones and even trees had a phallic significance, and for Bouvard and Pécuchet everything became phallic. They collected swing-poles of carriages, chair-legs, cellar bolts, pharmacists' pestles. When people came to see them they would ask: "What do you think that looks like?" then confided the mystery, and if there were objections, they shrugged their shoulders pityingly.[11]

Even in this subcategory of phallic objects, Flaubert maintains the heterogeneity of the museum's artifacts, a heterogeneity which defies the systematization and homogenization that knowledge demanded.

> The set of objects the *Museum* displays is sustained only by the fiction that they somehow constitute a coherent representational universe. The fiction is that a repeated metonymic displacement of fragment for totality, object to label, series of objects to series of labels, can still produce a representation which is somehow adequate to a nonlinguistic universe. Such a fiction is the result of an uncritical belief in the notion that ordering and classifying, that is to say, the spatial juxtaposition of fragments, can produce a representational understanding of the world. Should the fiction disappear, there is nothing left of the *Museum* but "bric-a-brac," a heap of meaningless and valueless fragments of objects which are incapable of substituting themselves either metonymically for the original objects or metaphorically for their representations.[12]

This view of the museum is what Flaubert figures through the comedy of *Bouvard and Pécuchet*. Founded on the disciplines of archeology and natural history, both inherited from the classical age, the museum was a discredited institution from its very inception. And the history of museology is a history of all the various attempts to deny the heterogeneity of the museum, to reduce it to a homogeneous system or series. The faith in the possibility of ordering the museum's "bric-a-brac," echoing that of Bouvard and Pécuchet themselves, persists until today. Reinstallations like that of the Metropolitan's 19th-century collection of the André Meyer

Galleries, particularly numerous throughout the past decade, are testimonies to that faith. What so alarmed Hilton Kramer in this particular instance is that the criterion for determining the order of aesthetic objects in the museum throughout the era of modernism—the "self-evident" quality of masterpieces—has been broken, and as a result "anything goes." Nothing could testify more eloquently to the fragility of the museum's claims to represent anything coherent at all.

In the period following World War II, perhaps the greatest monument to the museum's discourse is André Malraux's *Museum Without Walls*. If *Bouvard and Pécuchet* is a parody of received ideas of the mid-19th century, the *Museum Without Walls* is the hyperbole of such ideas in the mid-20th. Specifically, what Malraux unconsciously parodies is "art history as a humanistic discipline." For Malraux finds in the notion of style the ultimate homogenizing principle, indeed the essence of art, hypostatized, interestingly enough, through the medium of photography. Any work of art that can be photographed can take its place in Malraux's super-museum. But photography not only secures the admittance of objects, fragments of objects, details, etc., to the museum; it is also the organizing device: it reduces the now even vaster heterogeneity to a single perfect similitude. Through photographic reproduction a cameo takes up residence on the page next to a painted tondo and a sculpted relief; a detail of a Rubens in Antwerp is compared to that of a Michelangelo in Rome. The art historian's slide lecture, the art history student's slide comparison exam inhabit the museum without walls. In a recent example provided by one of our most eminent art historians, the oil sketch for a small detail of a cobblestone street in *Paris — A Rainy Day,* painted in the 1870s by Gustave Caillebotte, occupies the left-hand screen while a painting by Robert Ryman from the *Winsor* series of 1966 occupies the right, and presto! they are revealed to be one and the same.[13] But precisely what kind of knowledge is it that this artistic essence, style, can provide? Here is Malraux:

> Reproduction has disclosed the whole world's sculpture. It has multiplied accepted masterpieces, promoted other works to their due rank and launched some minor styles—in some cases, one might say, invented them. It is introducing the language of color into art history; in our Museum Without Walls, picture, fresco, miniature and stained-glass window seem of one and the same family. For all alike—miniatures, frescoes, stained glass, tapestries, Scythian plaques, pictures, Greek vase paintings, "details" and even statuary—have become "color-plates." In the process they have lost their properties as *objects;* but, by the same token, they have gained something: the utmost significance as to *style* that they can possibly acquire. It is hard for us clearly to realize the gulf between the performance of an Aeschylean tragedy, with the instant Persian threat and Salamis looming

across the Bay, and the effect we get from reading it; yet, dimly albeit, we feel the difference. All that remains of Aeschylus is his genius. It is the same with figures that in reproduction lose both their original significance as objects and their function (religious or other); we see them only as works of art and they bring home to us only their makers' talent. We might almost call them not "works" but "moments" of art. Yet diverse as they are, all these objects . . . speak for the same endeavor; it is as though an unseen presence, the spirit of art, were urging all on the same quest. . . . Thus it is that, thanks to the rather specious unity imposed by photographic reproduction on a multiplicity of objects, ranging from the statue to the bas-relief, from bas-reliefs to seal-impressions, and from these to the plaques of the nomads, a "Babylonian style" seems to emerge as a real entity, not a mere classification—as something resembling, rather, the life-story of a great creator. Nothing conveys more vividly and compellingly the notion of a destiny shaping human ends than do the great styles, whose evolutions and transformations seem like long scars that Fate has left, in passing, on the face of the earth.[14]

All of the works that we call art, or at least all of them that can be submitted to the process of photographic reproduction, can take their place in the great super-oeuvre, Art as ontological essence, created not by men in their historical contingencies, but by Man in his very being. This is the comforting "knowledge" to which the *Museum Without Walls* gives testimony. And concomitantly, it is the deception to which art history, a discipline now thoroughly professionalized, is most deeply, if often unconsciously, committed.

But Malraux makes a fatal error near the end of his *Museum:* he admits within its pages the very thing that had constituted its homogeneity; that thing is, of course, photography. So long as photography was merely a *vehicle* by which art objects entered the imaginary museum, a certain coherence obtained. But once photography itself enters, an object among others, heterogeneity is reestablished at the heart of the museum; its pretentions of knowledge are doomed. Even photography cannot hypostatize style from a photograph.

In Flaubert's "Dictionary of Received Ideas" the entry under "Photography" reads, "Will make painting obsolete. (See Daguerreotype.)" And the entry for "Daguerreotype" reads, in turn, "Will take the place of painting. (See Photography.)"[15] No one took seriously the possibility that photography might usurp painting. Less than half a century after photography's invention such a notion was one of those received ideas to be parodied. In our century until recently only Walter Benjamin gave credence to the notion, claiming that inevitably photography would have a truly profound effect upon art, even to the extent that the art of painting might disappear, having lost its all-important aura through mechanical reproduc-

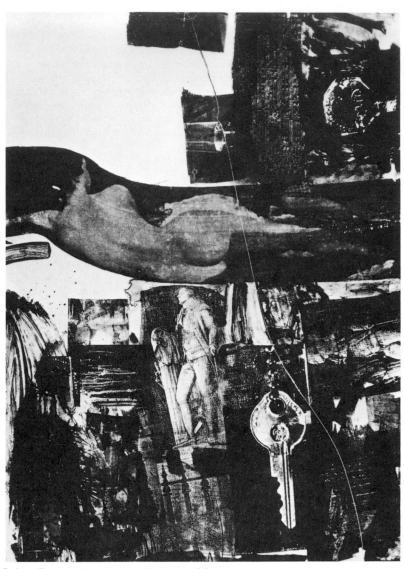

Robert Rauschenberg: *Break-Through*, 1964.

tion.[16] A denial of this power of photography to transform art continued to energize modernist painting through the immediate postwar period in America. But then in the work of Rauschenberg photography began to conspire with painting in its own destruction.[17]

While it was only with slight discomfort that Rauschenberg was called a painter throughout the first decade of his career, when he systematically embraced photographic images in the early '60s it became less and less possible to think of his work as painting. It was instead a hybrid form of *printing*. Rauschenberg had moved definitively from techniques of *production* (combines, assemblages) to techniques of *reproduction* (silkscreens, transfer drawings). And it is this move that requires us to think of Rauschenberg's art as postmodernist. Through reproductive technology postmodernist art dispenses with the aura. The fiction of the creating subject gives way to the frank confiscation, quotation, excerptation, accumulation and repetition of already existing images.[18] Notions of originality, authenticity and presence, essential to the ordered discourse of the museum, are undermined. Rauschenberg steals the *Rokeby Venus* and screens her onto the surface of *Crocus,* which also contains pictures of mosquitoes and a truck, as well as a reduplicated Cupid with a mirror. She appears again, twice, in *Transom,* now in the company of a helicopter and repeated images of water towers on Manhattan rooftops. In *Bicycle* she appears with the truck of *Crocus* and the helicopter of *Transom* but now also a sailboat, a cloud, an eagle. She reclines just above three Cunningham dancers in *Overcast III* and atop a statue of George Washington and a car key in *Breakthrough.* The absolute heterogeneity that is the purview of photography, and through photography, the museum, is spread across the surface of every Rauschenberg work. More importantly, it spreads from work to work.

Malraux was enraptured by the endless possibilities of his Museum, by the proliferation of discourses it could set in motion, establishing ever new series of iconography and style simply by reshuffling the photographs. That proliferation is enacted by Rauschenberg: Malraux's dream has become Rauschenberg's joke. But, of course, not everyone gets the joke, least of all Rauschenberg himself, judging from the proclamation he composed for the Metropolitan Museum's Centennial Certificate in 1970:

> Treasury of the conscience of man.
> Masterworks collected, protected and
> celebrated commonly. Timeless in
> concept the museum amasses to
> concertise a moment of pride
> serving to defend the dreams

and ideals apolitically of mankind
aware and responsive to the
changes, needs and complexities
of current life while keeping
history and love alive.

This certificate, containing photographic reproductions of works of art without the intrusion of anything else, was signed by the museum officials.

References

1. Hilton Kramer, "Does Gérôme Belong with Goya and Monet?" *New York Times,* April 13, 1980, section 2, p. 35.
2. Theodor W. Adorno, "Valéry Proust Museum," in *Prisms,* trans. Samuel and Shierry Weber (London: Neville Spearman, 1967), pp. 173-186.
3. Kramer, p. 35.
4. Leo Steinberg, "Other Criteria," in *Other Criteria* (New York: Oxford University Press, 1972), pp. 55-91. This essay is based on a lecture presented at the Museum of Modern Art, New York, in March 1968.
5. Ibid., p. 84.
6. See Rosalind Krauss's discussion of the radical difference between cubist collage and Rauschenberg's "reinvented" collage in "Rauschenberg and the Materialized Image," *Artforum,* XIII, 4 (December 1974), pp. 36-43.
7. Not all art historians would agree that Manet made the relationship of painting to its sources problematic. This is, however, the initial assumption of Michael Fried's "Manet's Sources: Aspects of his Art, 1859-1865" (*Artforum,* VII, 7 [March 1969], pp. 28-82), whose first sentence reads: "If a single question is guiding for our understanding of Manet's art during the first half of the 1860s, it is this: What are we to make of the numerous references in his paintings of those years to the work of the great painters of the past?" (p. 28). In part, Fried's presupposition that Manet's references to earlier art were *different,* in their "literalness and obviousness," from the ways in which Western painting had previously used sources led Theodore Reff to attack Fried's essay, saying, for example, "When Reynolds portrays his sitters in attitudes borrowed from famous pictures by Holbein, Michelangelo, and Annibale Carracci, wittily playing on their relevance to his own subjects; when Ingres deliberately refers in his religious compositions to those of Raphael, and in his portraits to familiar examples of Greek sculpture or Roman painting, do they not reveal the same historical consciousness that informs Manet's early work?" (Theodore Reff, "'Manet's Sources': A Critical Evaluation," *Artforum,* VIII, 1 [September 1969], p. 40). As a result of this denial of difference, Reff is able to continue applying to modernism art-historical methodologies devised to explain past art, for example that which explains the very particular relationship of Italian Renaissance art to the art of classical antiquity.

It was the parodic example of such blind application of art-historical methodology to the art of Rauschenberg that occasioned the present essay. In this instance, presented in a lecture by Robert Pincus-Witten, the source for Rauschenberg's *Monogram* (an assemblage which employs a stuffed angora goat) was said to be William Holman Hunt's *Scapegoat*!

8. Michel Foucault, "Fantasia of the Library," in *Language, Counter-Memory, Practice,* trans. Donald F. Bouchard and Sherry Simon (Ithaca: Cornell University Press), pp. 92-93.

9. Quoted in Eugenio Donato, "The Museum's Furnace: Notes Toward a Contextual Reading of *Bouvard and Pécuchet,*" in *Textual Strategies: Perspectives in Post-Structuralist Criticism,* ed. Josué V. Harari (Ithaca: Cornell University Press, 1979), p. 214. I wish to thank Rosalind Krauss for bringing Donato's essay to my attention, and more generally for her many helpful suggestions during the preparation of this text.

10. Ibid., p. 220. The apparent continuity between Foucault's and Donato's essays here is misleading, inasmuch as Donato is explicitly engaged in an attack upon Foucault's archeological methodology, claiming that it implicates Foucault in a return to a metaphysics of origins. Foucault himself moved beyond his "archeology" as soon as he had codified it in *The Archeology of Knowledge* (New York: Pantheon Books, 1969).

11. Gustave Flaubert, *Bouvard and Pécuchet,* trans. A.J. Krailsheimer (New York: Penguin Books, 1976), pp. 114-115.

12. Donato, p. 223.

13. This comparison was first presented by Robert Rosenblum in a symposium entitled "Modern Art and the Modern City: From Caillebotte and the Impressionists to the Present Day," held in conjunction with the Gustave Caillebotte exhibition at the Brooklyn Museum in March 1977. Rosenblum published a version of his lecture, although only works by Caillebotte were illustrated. The following excerpt will suffice to give an impression of the comparisons Rosenblum drew: "Caillebotte's art seems equally in tune with some of the structural innovations of recent nonfigurative painting and sculpture. His embracing, in the 1870s, of the new experience of modern Paris... involves fresh ways of seeing that are surprisingly close to our own decade. For one, he seems to have polarized more than any of his Impressionist contemporaries the extremities of the random and the ordered, usually juxtaposing these contrary modes in the same work. Parisians in city and country come and go in open spaces, but within their leisurely movements are grids of arithmetic, technological regularity. Crisscrossing or parallel patters of steel girders move with an A A A A beat along the railing of a bridge. Checkerboards of square pavement stones map out the repetitive grid systems we see in Warhol or early Stella, Ryman or Andre. Clean stripes, as in Daniel Buren[!], suddenly impose a cheerful, primary esthetic order upon urban flux and scatter." ("Gustave Caillebotte: The 1970s and the 1870s," *Artforum,* XV, 7 [March 1977], p. 52.) When Rosenblum again presented the Ryman-Caillebotte slide comparison in a symposium on modernism at Hunter College in March 1980, he admitted that it was perhaps what Panofsky would have called a pseudomorphism.

14. André Malraux, *The Voices of Silence* (Princeton: Princeton University Press, Bollingen Series XXIV, 1978), pp. 44, 46.

15. Flaubert, pp. 321, 300.

16. See Walter Benjamin, "The Work of Art in the Age of Mechanical Reproduction," in *Illuminations,* trans. Harry Zohn (New York: Schocken Books, 1969), pp. 217-251.

17. See my essay, "The End of Painting," *October* 16 (Spring 1981), pp. 69-86.

18. For further discussion of these postmodernist techniques pervasive in recent art, see my essays "Pictures," *October,* no. 8 (Spring 1979), pp. 67-86, and "The Photographic Activity of Postmodernism," *October,* no. 15 (Winter 1980), pp. 91-101. That we are now experiencing the "decay of the aura" that Benjamin predicted can be understood not only in these positive terms of what has replaced it, but also in the many desperate attempts to recuperate it by reviving the style and rhetoric of expressionism. This tendency is particularly strong in the marketplace but has also been wholeheartedly welcomed by the

museums. On the other hand, both museums and marketplace have also begun to "naturalize" the techniques of postmodernism, turning them into mere categories according to which a whole new range of heterogeneous objects can be organized. See my essay "Appropriating Appropriation" in *Image Scavengers: Photographs* (Philadelphia: Institute of Contemporary Art, 1982), pp. 27-34.

The Discourse of Others:
Feminists and Postmodernism

CRAIG OWENS

Postmodern knowledge [le savoir postmoderne] *is not simply an instrument of power. It refines our sensitivity to differences and increases our tolerance of incommensurability.* —J.F. Lyotard, *La condition postmoderne*

Decentered, allegorical, schizophrenic...—however we choose to diagnose its symptoms, postmodernism is usually treated, by its protagonists and antagonists alike, as a crisis of cultural authority, specifically of the authority vested in Western European culture and its institutions. That the hegemony of European civilization is drawing to a close is hardly a new perception; since the mid-1950s, at least, we have recognized the necessity of encountering different cultures by means other than the shock of domination and conquest. Among the relevant texts are Arnold Toynbee's discussion, in the eighth volume of his monumental *Study in History,* of the end of the modern age (an age that began, Toynbee contends, in the late 15th century when Europe began to exert its influence over vast land areas and populations not its own) and the beginning of a new, properly postmodern age characterized by the coexistence of different cultures. Claude Lévi-Strauss's critique of Western ethnocentrism could also be cited in this context, as well as Jacques Derrida's critique of this critique in *Of Grammatology.* But perhaps the most eloquent testimony to the end of Western sovereignty has been that of Paul Ricoeur, who wrote in 1962 that "the discovery of the plurality of cultures is never a harmless experience."

> When we discover that there are several cultures instead of just one and consequently at the time when we acknowledge the end of a sort of cultural monopoly, be it illusory or real, we are threatened with the destruction of our own discovery. Suddenly it becomes possible that there are just *others,* that we ourselves are an "other" among others. All meaning and every goal

having disappeared, it becomes possible to wander through civilizations as if through vestiges and ruins. The whole of mankind becomes an imaginary museum: where shall we go this weekend—visit the Angkor ruins or take a stroll in the Tivoli of Copenhagen? We can very easily imagine a time close at hand when any fairly well-to-do person will be able to leave his country indefinitely in order to taste his own national death in an interminable, aimless voyage.[1]

Lately, we have come to regard this condition as postmodern. Indeed, Ricoeur's account of the more dispiriting effects of our culture's recent loss of mastery anticipates both the melancholia and the eclecticism that pervade current cultural production—not to mention its much-touted pluralism. Pluralism, however, reduces us to being an other among others; it is not a recognition, but a reduction to difference to absolute indifference, equivalence, interchangeability (what Jean Baudrillard calls "implosion"). What is at stake, then, is not only the hegemony of Western culture, but also (our sense of) our identity as a culture. These two stakes, however, are so inextricably intertwined (as Foucault has taught us, the positing of an Other is a necessary moment in the consolidation, the incorporation of any cultural body) that it is possible to speculate that what has toppled our claims to sovereignty is actually the realization that our culture is neither as homogeneous nor as monolithic as we once believed it to be. In other words, the causes of modernity's demise—at least as Ricoeur describes its effects—lie as much within as without. Ricoeur, however, deals only with the difference without. What about the difference within?

In the modern period the authority of the work of art, its claim to represent some authentic vision of the world, did not reside in its uniqueness or singularity, as is often said; rather, that authority was based on the universality modern aesthetics attributed to the *forms* utilized for the representation of vision, over and above differences in content due to the production of works in concrete historical circumstances.[2] (For example, Kant's demand that the judgment of taste be universal—i.e., universally communicable—that it derive from "grounds deep-seated and shared alike by all men, underlying their agreement in estimating the forms under which objects are given to them.") Not only does the postmodernist work claim no such authority, it also actively seeks to undermine all such claims; hence, its generally deconstructive thrust. As recent analyses of the "enunciative apparatus" of visual representation—its poles of emission and reception— confirm, the representational systems of the West admit only one vision— that of the constitutive male subject—or, rather, they posit the subject of representation as absolutely centered, unitary, masculine.[3]

The postmodernist work attempts to upset the reassuring stability of that mastering position. This same project has, of course, been attributed by writers like Julia Kristeva and Roland Barthes to the *modernist* avant-garde, which through the introduction of heterogeneity, discontinuity, glossolalia, etc., supposedly put the subject of representation in crisis. But the avant-garde sought to transcend representation in favor of presence and imme-diacy; it proclaimed the autonomy of the signifier, its liberation from the "tyranny of the signified"; postmodernists instead expose the tyranny of the *signifier,* the violence of its law.[4] (Lacan spoke of the necessity of submitting to the "defiles" of the signifier; should we not ask rather who in our culture is defiled by the signifier?) Recently, Derrida has cautioned against a wholesale condemnation of representation, not only because such a condemnation may appear to advocate a rehabilitation of presence and immediacy and thereby serve the interests of the most reactionary political tendencies, but more importantly, perhaps, because that which exceeds, "transgresses the figure of all possible representation," may ultimately be none other than...the law. Which obliges us, Derrida concludes, "to thinking altogether *differently.*" [5]

It is precisely at the legislative frontier between what can be represented and what cannot that the postmodernist operation is being staged—not in order to transcend representation, but in order to expose that system of power that authorizes certain representations while blocking, prohibiting or invalidating others. Among those prohibited from Western representation, whose representations are denied all legitimacy, are women. Excluded from representation by its very structure, they return within it as a figure for—a representation of—the unrepresentable (Nature, Truth, the Sublime, etc.). This prohibition bears primarily on woman as the subject, and rarely as the object of representation, for there is certainly no shortage of images *of* women. Yet in being represented by, women have been rendered an absence within the dominant culture as Michèle Montrelay proposes when she asks "whether psychoanalysis was not articulated precisely in order to repress femininity (in the sense of producing its symbolic representation)." [6] In order to speak, to represent herself, a woman assumes a masculine position; perhaps this is why femininity is frequently associated with masquerade, with false representation, with simulation and seduction. Montrelay, in fact, identifies women as the "ruin of representation": not only have they nothing to lose; their exteriority to Western representation exposes its limits.

Here, we arrive at an apparent crossing of the feminist critique of patri-archy and the postmodernist critique of representation; this essay is a provisional attempt to explore the implications of that intersection. My intention is not to posit identity between these two critiques; nor is it to place them in a relation of antagonism or opposition. Rather, if I have chosen to negotiate the treacherous course between postmodernism and feminism, it is in order to introduce the issue of sexual difference into the modernism/postmodernism debate—a debate which has until now been scandalously in-different.[7]

"A Remarkable Oversight" [8]

Several years ago I began the second of two essays devoted to an allegorical impulse in contemporary art—an impulse that I identified as postmodernist —with a discussion of Laurie Anderson's multi-media performance *Americans on the Move*.[9] Addressed to transportation as a metaphor for communication—the transfer of meaning from one place to another— *Americans on the Move* proceeded primarily as verbal commentary on visual images projected on a screen behind the performers. Near the beginning Anderson introduced the schematic image of a nude man and woman, the former's right arm raised in greeting, that had been emblazoned on the Pioneer spacecraft. Here is what she had to say about this picture; significantly, it was spoken by a distinctly male voice (Anderson's own processed through a harmonizer, which dropped it an octave—a kind of electronic vocal transvestism):

> In our country, we send pictures of our sign language into outer space. They are speaking our sign language in these pictures. Do you think they will think his hand is permanently attached that way? Or do you think they will read our signs? In our country, good-bye looks just like hello.

Here is my commentary on this passage:

> Two alternatives: either the extraterrestrial recipient of this message will assume that it is simply a picture, that is, an analogical likeness of the human figure, in which case he might logically conclude that male inhabitants of Earth walk around with their right arms permanently raised. Or he will somehow divine that this gesture is addressed to him and attempt to read it, in which case he will be stymied, since a single gesture signifies both greeting and farewell, and any reading of it must oscillate between these two extremes. The same gesture could also mean "Halt!" or represent the taking of an oath, but if Anderson's text does not consider these two alternatives that is because it is not concerned with ambiguity, with multiple meanings engendered by a single sign; rather, two *clearly defined but mutually incompatible* readings are engaged in blind confrontation in such a way that it is impossible to choose between them.

This analysis strikes me as a case of gross critical negligence. For in my eagerness to rewrite Anderson's text in terms of the debate over determinate versus indeterminate meaning, I had overlooked something—something that is so obvious, so "natural" that it may at the time have seemed unworthy of comment. It does not seem that way to me today. For this is, of course, an image of sexual difference or, rather, of sexual differentiation according to the distribution of the phallus—as it is marked and then re-marked by the man's right arm, which appears less to have been raised than erected in greeting. I was, however, close to the "truth" of the image when I suggested that men on Earth might walk around with something permanently raised—close, perhaps, but no cigar. (Would my reading have been different—or less in-different—had I known then that, earlier in her career, Anderson had executed a work which consisted of photographs of men who had accosted her in the street?) [10] Like all representations of sexual difference that our culture produces, this is an image not simply of anatomical difference, but of the values assigned to it. Here, the phallus is a signifier (that is, it represents the subject for another signifier); it is, in fact, the privileged signifier, the signifier of privilege, of the power and prestige that accrue to the male in our society. As such, it designates the effects of signification in general. For in this (Lacanian) image, chosen to represent the inhabitants of Earth for the extraterrestrial Other, it is the man who speaks, who represents mankind. The woman is only represented; she is (as always) already spoken for.

If I return to this passage here, it is not simply to correct my own remarkable oversight, but more importantly to indicate a blind spot in our discussions of postmodernism in general: our failure to address the issue of sexual difference—not only in the objects we discuss, but in our own enunciation as well.[11] However restricted its field of inquiry may be, every discourse on postmodernism—at least insofar as it seeks to account for certain recent mutations within that field—aspires to the status of a general theory of contemporary culture. Among the most significant developments of the past decade—it may well turn out to have been *the* most significant—has been the emergence, in nearly every area of cultural activity, of a specifically feminist practice. A great deal of effort has been devoted to the recovery and revaluation of previously marginalized or underestimated work; everywhere this project has been accompanied by energetic new production. As one engaged in these activities—Martha Rosler—observes, they have contributed significantly to debunking the privileged status modernism claimed for the work of art: "The interpretation of the meaning and social origin and rootedness of those [earlier] forms helped undermine the modernist tenet of the separateness of the aesthetic from the rest of human life, and an analysis of the oppressiveness of the seemingly unmotivated forms of high culture was companion to this work." [12]

Still, if one of the most salient aspects of our postmodern culture is the presence of an insistent feminist voice (and I use the terms *presence* and *voice* advisedly), theories of postmodernism have tended either to neglect or to repress that voice. The absence of discussions of sexual difference in writings about postmodernism, as well as the fact that few women have engaged in the modernism/postmodernism debate, suggest that postmodernism may be another masculine invention engineered to exclude women. I would like to propose, however, that women's insistence on difference and incommensurability may not only be compatible with, but also an instance of postmodern thought. Postmodern thought is no longer binary thought (as Lyotard observes when he writes, "Thinking by means of oppositions does not correspond to the liveliest modes of postmodern knowledge [*le savoir postmoderne*]").[13] The critique of binarism is sometimes dismissed as intellectual fashion; it is, however, an intellectual imperative, since the hierarchical opposition of marked and unmarked terms (the decisive/divisive presence/absence of the phallus) is the dominant form both of representing difference and justifying its subordination in our society. What we must learn, then, is how to conceive difference without opposition.

Although sympathetic male critics respect feminism (an old theme: respect for women)[14] and wish it well, they have in general declined the dialogue in which their female colleagues are trying to engage them. Sometimes feminists are accused of going too far, at others, not far enough.[15] The feminist voice is usually regarded as one among many, its insistence on difference as testimony to the pluralism of the times. Thus, feminism is rapidly assimilated to a whole string of liberation or self-determination movements. Here is one recent list, by a prominent male critic: "ethnic groups, neighborhood movements, feminism, various 'countercultural' or alternative life-style groups, rank-and-file labor dissidence, student movements, single-issue movements." Not only does this forced coalition treat feminism itself as monolithic, thereby suppressing its multiple internal differences (essentialist, culturalist, linguistic, Freudian, anti-Freudian . . .); it also posits a vast, undifferentiated category, "Difference," to which all marginalized or oppressed groups can be assimilated, and for which women can then stand as an emblem, a *pars totalis* (another old theme: woman is incomplete, not whole). But the specificity of the feminist critique of patriarchy is thereby denied, along with that of all other forms of opposition to sexual, racial and class discrimination. (Rosler warns against using woman as "a token for all markers of difference," observing that "appreciation of the work of women whose subject is oppression exhausts consideration of all oppressions.")

Moreover, men appear unwilling to address the issues placed on the critical agenda by women unless those issues have first been neut(e)ralized —although this, too, is a problem of assimilation: to the already known, the already written. In *The Political Unconscious*, to take but one example, Fredric Jameson calls for the "reaudition of the oppositional voices of black and ethnic cultures, women's or gay literature, 'naive' or marginalized folk art *and the like*" (thus, women's cultural production is anachronistically identified as folk art), but he immediately modifies this petition: "The affirmation of such non-hegemonic cultural voices remains ineffective," he argues, if they are not first *rewritten* in terms of their proper place in "the dialogical system of the social classes."[16] Certainly, the class determinants of sexuality—and of sexual oppression—are too often overlooked. But sexual inequality cannot be reduced to an instance of economic exploitation —the exchange of women among men—and explained in terms of class struggle alone; to invert Rosler's statement, exclusive attention to economic oppression can exhaust consideration of other forms of oppression.

To claim that the division of the sexes is irreducible to the division of labor is to risk polarizing feminism and Marxism; this danger is real, given the latter's fundamentally patriarchal bias. Marxism privileges the characteristically masculine activity of production as the *definitively human* activity (Marx: men "begin to distinguish themselves from animals as soon as they begin to produce their means of subsistence");[17] women, historically consigned to the spheres of nonproductive or reproductive labor, are thereby situated outside the society of male producers, in a state of nature. (As Lyotard has written, "The frontier passing between the sexes does not separate two parts of the same social entity.")[18] What is at issue, however, is not simply the oppressiveness of Marxist discourse, but its totalizing ambitions, its claim to account for every form of social experience. But this claim is characteristic of all theoretical discourse, which is one reason women frequently condemn it as phallocratic.[19] It is not always theory *per se* that women repudiate, nor simply, as Lyotard has suggested, the priority men have granted to it, its rigid opposition to practical experience. Rather, what they challenge is the distance it maintains between itself and its objects—a distance which objectifies and masters.

Because of the tremendous effort of reconceptualization necessary to prevent a phallologic relapse in their own discourse, many feminist artists have, in fact, forged a new (or renewed) alliance with theory—most profitably, perhaps, with the writing of women influenced by Lacanian psychoanalysis (Luce Irigaray, Hélène Cixous, Montrelay...). Many of these artists have themselves made major theoretical contributions: filmmaker Laura Mulvey's 1975 essay on "Visual Pleasure and Narrative Cinema," for example, has generated a great deal of critical discussion on the masculinity of the cinematic gaze.[20] Whether influenced by psychoanalysis or not, feminist artists often regard critical or theoretical writing as an important arena of strategic intervention: Martha Rosler's critical texts on the documentary tradition in photography—among the best in the field— are a crucial part of her activity *as an artist*. Many modernist artists, of course, produced texts about their own production, but writing was almost always considered supplementary to their primary work as painters, sculptors, photographers, etc.,[21] whereas the kind of simultaneous activity on multiple fronts that characterizes many feminist practices is a postmodern phenomenon. And one of the things it challenges is modernism's rigid opposition of artistic practice and theory.

At the same time, postmodern feminist practice may question theory—

and not only *aesthetic* theory. Consider Mary Kelly's *Post-Partum Document* (1973-79), a 6-part, 165-piece art work (plus footnotes) that utilizes multiple representational modes (literary, scientific, psychoanalytic, linguistic, archeological and so forth) to chronicle the first six years of her son's life. Part archive, part exhibition, part case history, the *Post-Partum Document* is also a contribution to as well as a critique of Lacanian theory. Beginning as it does with a series of diagrams taken from *Ecrits* (diagrams which Kelly presents as *pictures*), the work might be (mis)read as a straightforward application or illustration of psychoanalysis. It is, rather, a mother's interrogation of Lacan, an interrogation that ultimately reveals a remarkable oversight within the Lacanian narrative of the child's relation to the mother—the construction of the mother's fantasies vis-à-vis the child. Thus, the *Post-Partum Document* has proven to be a controversial work, for it appears to offer evidence of *female* fetishism (the various substitutes the mother invests in order to disavow separation from the child); Kelly thereby exposes a lack within the theory of fetishism, a perversion heretofore reserved for the male. Kelly's work is not anti-theory; rather, as her use of multiple representational systems testifies, it demonstrates that no one narrative can possibly account for all aspects of human experience. Or as the artist herself has said, "There's no single theoretical discourse which is going to offer an explanation for all forms of social relations or for every mode of political practice." [22]

A la recherche du récit perdu

"No single theoretical discourse..."—this feminist position is also a postmodern condition. In fact, Lyotard diagnoses *the* postmodern condition as one in which the *grands récits* of modernity—the dialectic of Spirit, the emancipation of the worker, the accumulation of wealth, the classless society—have all lost credibility. Lyotard defines a discourse as modern when it appeals to one or another of these *grands récits* for its legitimacy; the advent of postmodernity, then, signals a crisis in narrative's legitimizing function, its ability to compel consensus. Narrative, he argues, is out of its element(s)—"the great dangers, the great journeys, the great goal." Instead, "it is dispersed into clouds of linguistic particles—narrative ones, but also denotative, prescriptive, descriptive, etc.—each with its own pragmatic valence. Today, each of us lives in the vicinity of many of these. We do not necessarily form stable linguistic communities, and the properties of those we do form are not necessarily communicable." [23]

Lyotard does not, however, mourn modernity's passing, even though his own activity as a philosopher is at stake. "For most people," he writes, "nostalgia for the lost narrative [*le récit perdu*] is a thing of the past."[24] "Most people" does not include Fredric Jameson, although he diagnoses the postmodern condition in similar terms (as a loss of narrative's social function) and distinguishes between modernist and postmodernist works according to their different relations to the "'truth-content' of art, its claim to possess some truth or epistemological value." His description of a crisis in modernist literature stands metonymically for the crisis in modernity itself:

> At its most vital, the experience of modernism was not one of a single historical movement or process, but of a "shock of discovery," a commitment and an adherence to its individual forms through a series of "religious conversions." One did not simply read D.H. Lawrence or Rilke, see Jean Renoir or Hitchcock, or listen to Stravinsky as distinct manifestations of what we now term modernism. Rather one read all the works of a particular writer, learned a style and a phenomenological world, to which one converted.... This meant, however, that the experience of one form of modernism was incompatible with another, so that one entered one world only at the price of abandoning another....The crisis of modernism came, then, when it suddenly became clear that "D.H. Lawrence" was not an absolute after all, not the final achieved figuration of the truth of the world, but only one art-language among others, only one shelf of works in a whole dizzying library.[25]

Although a reader of Foucault might locate this realization at the origin of modernism (Flaubert, Manet) rather than at its conclusion,[26] Jameson's account of the crisis of modernity strikes me as both persuasive and problematic—problematic because persuasive. Like Lyotard, he plunges us into a radical Nietzschean perspectivism: each oeuvre represents not simply a different view of the same world, but corresponds to an entirely different world. Unlike Lyotard, however, he does so only in order to extricate us from it. For Jameson, the loss of narrative is equivalent to the loss of our ability to locate ourselves historically; hence, his diagnosis of postmodernism as "schizophrenic," meaning that it is characterized by a collapsed sense of temporality.[27] Thus, in *The Political Unconscious* he urges the resurrection not simply of narrative—as a "socially symbolic act"—but specifically of what he identifies as the Marxist "master narrative"—the story of mankind's "collective struggle to wrest a realm of Freedom from a realm of Necessity."[28]

Master narrative—how else to translate Lyotard's *grand récit*? And in this translation we glimpse the terms of another analysis of modernity's demise, one that speaks not of the incompatibility of the various modern narratives, but instead of their fundamental solidarity. For what made the *grands récits* of modernity master narratives if not the fact that they were all narratives of mastery, of man seeking his telos in the conquest of nature? What function did these narratives play other than to legitimize Western man's self-appointed mission of transforming the entire planet in his own image? And what form did this mission take if not that of man's placing of his stamp on everything that exists—that is, the transformation of the world into a representation, with man as its subject? In this respect, however, the phrase *master narrative* seems tautologous, since all narrative, by virtue of "its power to master the dispiriting effects of the corrosive force of the temporal process,"[29] may be narrative of mastery.[30]

What is at stake, then, is not only the status of narrative, but of representation itself. For the modern age was not only the age of the master narrative, it was also the age of representation—at least this is what Martin Heidegger proposed in a 1938 lecture delivered in Freiburg im Breisgau, but not published until 1952 as "The Age of the World Picture" [*Die Zeit die Weltbildes*].[31] According to Heidegger, the transition to modernity was not accomplished by the replacement of a medieval by a modern world picture, "but rather the fact that the world becomes a picture at all is what distinguishes the essence of the modern age." For modern man, everything that exists does so only in and through representation. To claim this is also to claim that the world exists only in and through a *subject* who believes that he is producing the world in producing its representation:

> The fundamental event of the modern age is the conquest of the world as picture. The word "picture" [*Bild*] now means the structured image [*Gebild*] that is the creature of man's producing which represents and sets before. In such producing, man contends for the position in which he can be that particular being who gives the measure and draws up the guidelines for everything that is.

Thus, with the "interweaving of these two events"—the transformation of the world into a picture and man into a subject—"there begins that way of being human which mans the realm of human capability given over to measuring and executing, for the purpose of gaining mastery of that which is as a whole." For what is representation if not a "laying hold and grasping" (appropriation), a "making-stand-over-against, an objectifying that goes forward and masters"?[32]

Thus, when in a recent interview Jameson calls for "the *reconquest* of certain forms of representation" (which he equates with narrative: "'Narrative,'" he argues, "is, I think, generally what people have in mind when they rehearse the usual post-structuralist 'critique of representation'"),[33] he is in fact calling for the rehabilitation of the entire social project of modernity itself. Since the Marxist master narrative is only one version among many of the modern narrative of mastery (for what is the "collective struggle to wrest a realm of Freedom from a realm of Necessity" if not mankind's progressive exploitation of the Earth?), Jameson's desire to resurrect (this) narrative is a modern desire, a desire *for* modernity. It is one symptom of our postmodern condition, which is experienced everywhere today as a tremendous loss of mastery and thereby gives rise to therapeutic programs, from both the Left and the Right, for recuperating that loss. Although Lyotard warns—correctly, I believe—against explaining transformations in modern/postmodern culture primarily as effects of social transformations (the hypothetical advent of a postindustrial society, for example),[34] it is clear that what has been lost is not primarily a cultural mastery, but an economic, technical and political one. For what if not the emergence of Third-World nations, the "revolt of nature" and the women's movement—that is, the voices of the conquered—has challenged the West's desire for ever-greater domination and control?

Symptoms of our recent loss of mastery are everywhere apparent in cultural activity today—nowhere more so than in the visual arts. The modernist project of joining forces with science and technology for the transformation of the environment after rational principles of function and utility (Productivism, the Bauhaus) has long since been abandoned; what we witness in its place is a desperate, often hysterical attempt to recover some sense of mastery via the resurrection of heroic large-scale easel painting and monumental cast-bronze sculpture—mediums themselves identified with the cultural hegemony of Western Europe. Yet contemporary artists are able at best to *simulate* mastery, to manipulate its signs, since in the modern period mastery was invariably associated with human labor, aesthetic production has degenerated today into a massive deployment of the signs of artistic labor—violent, "impassioned" brushwork, for example. Such simulacra of mastery testify, however, only to its loss; in fact, contemporary artists seem engaged in a collective act of disavowal—and disavowal always pertains to a loss ... of virility, masculinity, potency.[35]

This contingent of artists is accompanied by another which refuses the simulation of mastery in favor of melancholic contemplation of its loss. One such artist speaks of "the impossibility of passion in a culture that has institutionalized self-expression;" another, of "the aesthetic as something which is really about longing and loss rather than completion." A painter unearths the discarded genre of landscape painting only to borrow for his own canvases, through an implicit equation between their ravaged surfaces and the barren fields he depicts, something of the exhaustion of the earth itself (which is thereby glamorized); another dramatizes his anxieties through the most conventional figure men have conceived for the threat of castration—Woman ... aloof, remote, unapproachable. Whether they disavow or advertise their own powerlessness, pose as heroes or as victims, these artists have, needless to say, been warmly received by a society unwilling to admit that it has been driven from its position of centrality; theirs is an "official" art which, like the culture that produced it, has yet to come to terms with its own impoverishment.

Above and right: Martha Rosler, *The Bowery in Two Inadequate Descriptive Systems,* 1974-75.

Postmodernist artists speak of impoverishment—but in a very different way. Sometimes the postmodernist work testifies to a deliberate *refusal* of mastery, for example, Martha Rosler's *The Bowery in Two Inadequate Descriptive Systems* (1974-75), in which photographs of Bowery storefronts alternate with clusters of typewritten words signifying inebriety. Although her photographs are intentionally flat-footed, Rosler's refusal of mastery in this work is more than technical. On the one hand, she denies the caption/ text its conventional function of supplying the image with something it lacks; instead, her juxtaposition of two representational systems, visual and verbal, is calculated (as the title suggests) to "undermine" rather than "underline" the truth value of each.[36] More importantly, Rosler has refused to photograph the inhabitants of Skid Row, to speak on their behalf, to illuminate them from a safe distance (photography as social work in the tradition of Jacob Riis). For "concerned" or what Rosler calls "victim" photography overlooks the constitutive role of its own activity, which is held

plastered   stuccoed

rosined   shellacked

vulcanized

inebriated

polluted

to be merely representative (the "myth" of photographic transparency and objectivity). Despite his or her benevolence in representing those who have been denied access to the means of representation, the photographer inevitably functions as an agent of the system of power that silenced these people in the first place. Thus, they are twice victimized: first by society, and then by the photographer who presumes the right to speak on their behalf. In fact, in such photography it is the photographer rather than the "subject" who poses—as the subject's consciousness, indeed, as conscience itself. Although Rosler may not, in this work, have initiated a counter-discourse of drunkenness—which would consist of the drunks' own theories about their conditions of existence—she has nevertheless pointed negatively to the crucial issue of a politically motivated art practice today: "the indignity of speaking for others." [37]

Rosler's position poses a challenge to criticism as well, specifically, to the critic's substitution of his own discourse for the work of art. At this point in my text, then, my own voice must yield to the artist's; in the essay "in, around and afterthoughts (on documentary photography)" which accompanies *The Bowery* ... , Rosler writes:

> If impoverishment is a subject here, it is more certainly the impoverishment of representational strategies tottering about alone than that of a mode of surviving. The photographs are powerless to *deal with* the reality that is yet totally comprehended-in-advance by ideology, and they are as diversionary as the word formations—which at least are closer to being located within the culture of drunkenness rather than being framed on it from without.[38]

The Visible and the Invisible

A work like *The Bowery in Two Inadequate Descriptive Systems* not only exposes the "myths" of photographic objectivity and transparency; it also upsets the (modern) belief in vision as a privileged means of access to certainty and truth ("Seeing is believing"). Modern aesthetics claimed that vision was superior to the other senses because of its detachment from its objects: "Vision," Hegel tells us in his *Lectures on Aesthetics,* "finds itself in a purely theoretical relationship with objects, through the intermediary of light, that immaterial matter which truly leaves objects their freedom, lighting and illuminating them without consuming them." [39] Postmodernist artists do not deny this detachment, but neither do they celebrate it. Rather, they investigate the particular interests it serves. For vision is hardly disinterested; nor is it indifferent, as Luce Irigaray has observed: "Investment in the look is not privileged in women as in men. More than the other senses, the eye objectifies and masters. It sets at a distance, maintains the distance. In our culture, the predominance of the look over smell, taste, touch, hearing, has brought about an impoverishment of bodily relations.... The moment the look dominates, the body loses its materiality." [40] That is, it is transformed into an image.

That the priority our culture grants to vision is a sensory impoverishment is hardly a new perception; the feminist critique, however, links the privileging of vision with sexual privilege. Freud identified the transition from a matriarchal to a patriarchal society with the simultaneous devaluation of an olfactory sexuality and promotion of a more mediated, sublimated visual sexuality.[41] What is more, in the Freudian scenario it is by looking that the child discovers sexual difference, the presence or absence of the phallus according to which the child's sexual identity will be assumed. As Jane Gallop reminds us in her recent book *Feminism and Psychoanalysis: The Daughter's Seduction,* "Freud articulated the 'discovery of castration' around a sight: sight of a phallic presence in the boy, sight of a phallic absence in the girl, ultimately sight of a phallic absence in the mother. *Sexual difference takes its decisive significance from a sighting.*[42] Is it not because the phallus is the most visible sign of sexual difference that it has become the "privileged signifier"? However, it is not only the discovery of difference, but also its denial that hinges upon vision (although the reduction of difference to a common measure—woman judged according to the man's standard and found lacking—is already a denial). As Freud proposed in his 1926 paper on "Fetishism," the male child often takes the last visual impression prior to the "traumatic" sighting as a substitute for the mother's "missing" penis:

> Thus the foot or the shoe owes its attraction as a fetish, or part of it, to the circumstance that the inquisitive boy used to peer up at the woman's legs towards her genitals. Velvet and fur reproduce—as has long been suspected —the sight of the pubic hair which ought to have revealed the longed-for penis; the underlinen so often adopted as a fetish reproduces the scene of undressing, the last moment in which the woman could still be regarded as phallic.[43]

What can be said about the visual arts in a patriarchal order that privileges vision over the other senses? Can we not expect them to be a domain of masculine privilege—as their histories indeed prove them to be—a means, perhaps, of mastering through representation the "threat" posed by the female? In recent years there has emerged a visual arts practice informed by feminist theory and addressed, more or less explicitly, to the issue of representation and sexuality—both masculine and feminine. Male artists have tended to investigate the social construction of masculinity (Mike Glier, Eric Bogosian, the early work of Richard Prince); women have begun the long-overdue process of deconstructing femininity. Few have produced new, "positive" images of a revised femininity; to do so would simply supply and thereby prolong the life of the existing representational apparatus. Some refuse to represent women at all, believing that no representation of the female body in our culture can be free from phallic prejudice. Most of these artists, however, work with the existing repertory of cultural imagery not because they either lack originality or criticize it—but because their subject, feminine sexuality, is always constituted in and as representation, a representation of difference. It must be emphasized that these artists are not primarily interested in what representations say about women; rather, they investigate what representation *does* to women (for example, the way it invariably positions them as objects of the male gaze). For, as Lacan wrote, "Images and symbols *for* the woman cannot be isolated from images and symbols *of* the woman. . . . It is representation, the representation of feminine sexuality whether repressed or not, which conditions how it comes into play."[44]

Critical discussions of this work have, however, assiduously avoided—
skirted—the issue of gender. Because of its generally deconstructive
ambition, this practice is sometimes assimilated to the modernist tradition of
demystification. (Thus, the critique of representation is this work is
collapsed into ideological critique.) In an essay devoted (again) to
allegorical procedures in contemporary art, Benjamin Buchloh discusses the
work of six women artists—Dara Birnbaum, Jenny Holzer, Barbara
Kruger, Louise Lawler, Sherrie Levine, Martha Rosler—claiming them for
the model of "secondary mythification" elaborated in Roland Barthes's
1957 *Mythologies*. Buchloh does not acknowledge the fact that Barthes later
repudiated this methodology—a repudiation that must be seen as part of his
increasing refusal of mastery from *The Pleasure of the Text* on.[45] Nor does
Buchloh grant any particular significance to the fact that all these artists are
women; instead, he provides them with a distinctly male genealogy in the
dada tradition of collage and montage. Thus, all six artists are said to
manipulate the languages of popular culture—television, advertising,
photography—in such a way that "their ideological functions and effects
become *transparent*;" or again, in their work, "the minute and seemingly
inextricable interaction of behavior and ideology" supposedly becomes an
"*observable* pattern." [46]

But what does it mean to claim that these artists render the invisible
visible, especially in a culture in which visibility is always on the side of the
male, invisibility on the side of the female? And what is the critic really
saying when he states that these artists reveal, expose, "unveil" (this last
word is used throughout Buchloh's text) hidden ideological agendas in
mass-cultural imagery? Consider, for the moment, Buchloh's discussion of
the work of Dara Birnbaum, a video artist who re-edits footage taped
directly from broadcast television. Of Birnbaum's *Technology/Trans-
formation: Wonder Woman* (1978-79), based on the popular television series
of the same name, Buchloh writes that it "unveils the puberty fantasy of
Wonder Woman." Yet, like all of Birnbaum's work, this tape is dealing not
simply with mass-cultural imagery, but with mass-cultural *images of
women*. Are not the activities of unveiling, stripping, laying bare in relation
to a female body unmistakably male prerogatives?[47] Moreover, the women
Birnbaum re-presents are usually athletes and performers absorbed in the
display of their own physical perfection. They are without defect, without
lack, and therefore with neither history nor desire. (Wonder Woman is the
perfect embodiment of the phallic mother.) What we recognize in her work
is the Freudian trope of the narcissistic woman, or the Lacanian "theme" of
femininity as contained spectacle, which exists only as a representation of
masculine desire.[48]

The deconstructive impulse that animates this work has also suggested
affinities with poststructuralist textual strategies, and much of the critical

writing about these artists—including my own—has tended simply to translate their work into French. Certainly, Foucault's discussion of the West's strategies of marginalization and exclusion, Derrida's charges of "phallocentrism," Deleuze and Guattari's "body without organs" would all seem to be congenial to a feminist perspective. (As Irigaray has observed, is not the "body without organs" the historical condition of woman?)[49] Still, the affinities between poststructuralist theories and postmodernist practice can blind a critic to the fact that, when women are concerned, similar techniques have very different meanings. Thus, when Sherrie Levine appropriates—literally takes—Walker Evans's photographs of the rural poor or, perhaps more pertinently, Edward Weston's photographs of his son Neil posed as a classical Greek torso, is she simply dramatizing the diminished possibilities for creativity in an image-saturated culture, as is often repeated? Or is her refusal of authorship not in fact a refusal of the role of creator as "father" of his work, of the paternal rights assigned to the author by law?[50] (This reading of Levine's strategies is supported by the fact that the images she appropriates are invariably images of the Other: women, nature, children, the poor, the insane....)[51] Levine's disrespect for paternal authority suggests that her activity is less one of appropriation—a laying hold and grasping—and more one of expropriation: she expropriates the appropriators.

Sometimes Levine collaborates with Louise Lawler under the collective title "A Picture is No Substitute for Anything"—an unequivocal critique of representation as traditionally defined. (E.H. Gombrich: "All art is image-making, and all image-making is the creation of substitutes.") Does not their collaboration move us to ask what the picture is supposedly a substitute for, what it replaces, what absence it conceals? And when Lawler shows "A Movie without the Picture," as she did in 1979 in Los Angeles and again in 1983 in New York, is she simply soliciting the spectator as a collaborator in the production of the image? Or is she not also denying the viewer the kind of visual pleasure which cinema customarily provides—a pleasure that has been linked with the masculine perversions voyeurism and scopophilia?[52] It seems fitting, then, that in Los Angeles she screened (or didn't screen) *The Misfits*—Marilyn Monroe's last completed film. So that what Lawler withdrew was not simply a picture, but the archetypal image of feminine desirability.

When Cindy Sherman, in her untitled black-and-white studies for film stills (made in the late '70s and early '80s), first costumed herself to resemble heroines of grade-B Hollywood films of the late '50s and early '60s and then photographed herself in situations suggesting some immanent danger lurking just beyond the frame, was she simply attacking the rhetoric of "auteurism by equating the known artifice of the actress in front of the camera with the supposed authenticity of the director behind it"?[53] Or was

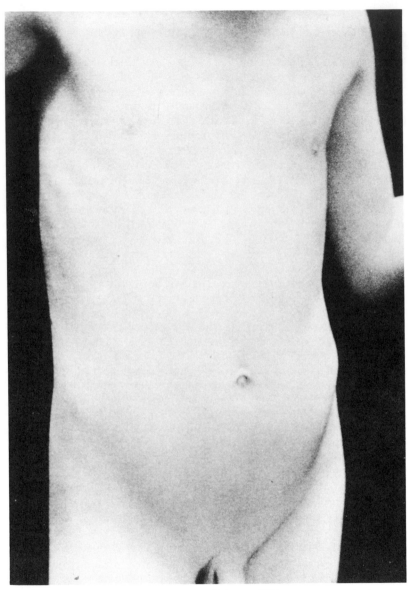

Sherrie Levine, *Photograph after Edward Weston*, 1980.

Cindy Sherman, *Untitled Film Still*, 1980.

her play-acting not also an acting out of the psychoanalytic notion of femininity as masquerade, that is, as a representation of male desire? As Hélène Cixous has written, "One is always in representation, and when a woman is asked to take place in this representation, she is, of course, asked to represent man's desire." [54] Indeed, Sherman's photographs themselves function as mirror-masks that reflect back at the viewer his own desire (and the spectator posited by this work is invariably male) — specifically, the masculine desire to fix the woman in a stable and stabilizing identity. But this is precisely what Sherman's work denies: for while her photographs are always self-portraits, in them the artist never appears to be the same, indeed, not even the same model; while we can presume to recognize the same person, we are forced at the same time to recognize a trembling around the edges of that identity.[55] In a subsequent series of works, Sherman abandoned the film-still format for that of the magazine centerfold, opening herself to charges that she was an accomplice in her own objectification, reinforcing the image of the woman bound by the frame.[56] This may be true; but while Sherman may pose as a pin-up, she still cannot be pinned down.

  Finally, when Barbara Kruger collages the words "Your gaze hits the side of my face" over an image culled from a '50s photo-annual of a female bust, is she simply "making an equation... between aesthetic reflection and the

Barbara Kruger, 1981.

alienation of the gaze: both reify"?[57] Or is she not speaking instead of the *masculinity* of the look, the ways in which it objectifies and masters? Or when the words "You invest in the divinity of the masterpiece" appear over a blown-up detail of the creation scene from the Sistine ceiling, is she simply parodying our reverence for works of art, or is this not a commentary on artistic production as a contract between fathers and sons? The address of Kruger's work is always gender-specific; her point, however, is not that masculinity and femininity are fixed positions assigned in advance by the representational apparatus. Rather, Kruger uses a term with no fixed content, the linguistic shifter ("I/you"), in order to demonstrate that masculine and feminine themselves are not stable identities, but subject to ex-change.

There is irony in the fact that all these practices, as well as the theoretical work that sustains them, have emerged in a historical situation supposedly characterized by its complete indifference. In the visual arts we have witnessed the gradual dissolution of once fundamental distinctions— original/copy, authentic/inauthentic, function/ornament. Each term now seems to contain its opposite, and this indeterminacy brings with it an impossibility of choice or, rather, the absolute equivalence and hence interchangeability of choices. Or so it is said.[58] The existence of feminism, with its insistence on difference, forces us to reconsider. For in our country good-bye may look just like hello, but only from a masculine position. Women have learned—perhaps they have always known—how to recognize the difference.

References

1. Paul Ricoeur, "Civilization and National Cultures," *History and Truth*, trans. Chas. A. Kelbley (Evanston: Northwestern University Press, 1965), p. 278.
2. Hayden White, "Getting Out of History," *diacritics*, 12, 3 (Fall 1982), p. 3. Nowhere does White acknowledge that it is precisely this universality that is in question today.
3. See, for example, Louis Marin, "Toward A Theory of Reading in the Visual Arts: Poussin's *The Arcadian Shepherds*," in S. Suleiman and I. Crosman, eds., *The Reader in the Text* (Princeton: Princeton University Press, 1980), pp. 293-324. This essay reiterates the main points of the first section of Marin's *Détruire le peinture* (Paris: Galilée, 1977). See also Christian Metz's discussion of the enunciative apparatus of cinematic representation in his "History/Discourse: A Note on Two Voyeurisms" in *The Imaginary Signifier*, trans. Britton, Williams, Brewster and Guzzetti (Bloomington: Indiana University Press, 1982). And for a general survey of these analyses, see my "Representation, Appropriation & Power," *Art in America*, 70, 5 (May 1982), pp. 9-21.
4. Hence Kristeva's problematic identification of avant-garde practice as feminine—problematic because it appears to act in complicity with all those discourses which exclude women from the order of representation, associating them instead with the presymbolic (Nature, the Unconscious, the body, etc.).
5. Jacques Derrida, "Sending: On Representation," trans. P. and M.A. Caws, *Social Research*, 49, 2 (Summer 1982), pp. 325, 326, italics added. (In this essay Derrida is discussing Heidegger's "The Age of the World Picture," a text to which I will return.) "Today there is a great deal of thought against representation," Derrida writes. "In a more or less articulated or rigorous way, this judgment is easily arrived at: representation is bad.... And yet, whatever the strength and the obscurity of this dominant current, the authority of representation constrains us, imposing itself on our thought through a whole dense, enigmatic, and heavily stratified history. It programs us and precedes us and warns us too severely for us to make a mere object of it, a representation, an object of representation confronting us, before us like a theme" (p. 304). Thus, Derrida concludes that "the essence of representation is not a representation, it is not representable, *there is no representation of representation*" (p. 314, italics added).
6. Michèle Montrelay, "Recherches sur la femininité," *Critique*, 278 (July 1970); translated by Parveen Adams as "Inquiry into Femininity," *m/f*, 1 (1978); repr. in *Semiotext(e)*, 10 (1981), p. 232.
7. Many of the issues treated in the following pages—the critique of binary thought, for example, or the privileging of vision over the other senses—have had long careers in the history of philosophy. I am interested, however, in the ways in which feminist theory articulates them onto the issue of sexual privilege. Thus, issues frequently condemned as merely epistemological turn out to be political as well. (For an example of this kind of condemnation, see Andreas Huyssens, "Critical Theory and Modernity," *New German Critique*, 26 [Spring/Summer 1982], pp. 3-11.) In fact, feminism demonstrates the impossibility of maintaining the split between the two.
8. "What is unquestionably involved here is a conceptual foregrounding of the sexuality of the woman, which brings to our attention a remarkable oversight." Jacques Lacan, "Guiding Remarks for a Congress on Feminine Sexuality," in J. Mitchell and J. Rose, eds., *Feminine Sexuality* (New York: Norton and Pantheon, 1982), p. 87.
9. See my "The Allegorical Impulse: Toward a Theory of Postmodernism" (part 2), *October*, 13 (Summer 1980), pp. 59-80. *Americans on the Move* was first performed at The Kitchen Center for Video, Music, and Dance in New York City in April 1979; it has since been revised and incorporated into Anderson's two-evening work *United States, Parts I-IV*, first seen in its entirety in February 1983 at the Brooklyn Academy of Music.
10. This project was brought to my attention by Rosalyn Deutsche.

11. As Stephen Heath writes, "Any discourse which fails to take account of the problem of sexual difference in its own enunciation and address will be, within a patriarchal order, precisely indifferent, a reflection of male domination." "Difference," *Screen*, 19, 4 (Winter 1978-79), p. 53.

12. Martha Rosler, "Notes on Quotes," *Wedge*, 2 (Fall 1982), p. 69.

13. Jean-Francois Lyotard, *La condition postmoderne* (Paris: Minuit, 1979), p. 29.

14. See Sarah Kofman, *Le Respect des femmes* (Paris: Galilée, 1982). A partial English translation appears as "The Economy of Respect: Kant and Respect for Women," trans. N. Fisher, *Social Research*, 49, 2 (Summer 1982), pp. 383-404.

15. Why is it always a question of *distance*? For example, Edward Said writes, "Nearly everyone producing literary or cultural studies mades no allowance for the truth that all intellectual or cultural work occurs somewhere, at some times, on some very precisely mapped-out and permissible terrain, which is ultimately contained by the State. Feminist critics have opened this question part of the way, but *they have not gone the whole distance*." "American 'Left' Literary Criticism," *The World, the Text, and the Critic* (Cambridge: Harvard University Press, 1983), p. 169. Italics added.

16. Fredric Jameson, *The Political Unconscious* (Ithaca: Cornell University Press, 1981), p. 84.

17. Marx and Engels, *The German Ideology* (New York: International Publishers, 1970), p. 42. One of the things that feminism has exposed is Marxism's scandalous blindness to sexual inequality. Both Marx and Engels viewed patriarchy as part of a precapitalist mode of production, claiming that the transition from a feudal to a capitalist mode of production was a transition from male domination to domination by capital. Thus, in the *Communist Manifesto* they write, "The bourgeoisie, wherever it has got the upper hand, has put an end to all feudal, patriarchal...relations." The revisionist attempt (such as Jameson proposes in *The Political Unconscious*) to explain the persistence of patriarchy as a survival of a previous mode of production is an inadequate response to the challenge posed by feminism to Marxism. Marxism's difficulty with feminism is not part of an ideological bias inherited from outside; rather, it is a structural effect of its privileging of production as the definitively human activity. On these problems, see Isaac D. Balbus, *Marxism and Domination* (Princeton: Princeton University Press, 1982), especially chapter 2, "Marxist Theories of Patriarchy," and chapter 5, "Neo-Marxist Theories of Patriarchy." See also Stanley Aronowitz, *The Crisis in Historical Materlalism* (Brooklyn: J.F. Bergin, 1981), especially chapter 4, "The Question of Class."

18. Lyotard, "One of the Things at Stake in Women's Struggles," *Substance*, 20 (1978), p. 15.

19. Perhaps the most vociferous feminist antitheoretical statement is Marguerite Duras's: "The criterion on which men judge intelligence is still the capacity to theorize and in all the movements that one sees now, in whatever area it may be, cinema, theater, literature, the theoretical sphere is losing influence. It has been under attack for centuries. It ought to be crushed by now, it should lose itself in a reawakening of the senses, blind itself, and be still." In E. Marks and I. de Courtivron, eds., *New French Feminisms* (New York: Schocken, 1981), p. 111. The implicit connection here between the privilege men grant to theory and that which they grant to vision over the other senses recalls the etymology of *theoria*; see below.

Perhaps it is more accurate to say that most feminists are ambivalent about theory. For example, in Sally Potter's film *Thriller* (1979)—which addresses the question "Who is responsible for Mimi's death?" in *La Bohème*—the heroine breaks out laughing while reading aloud from Kristeva's introduction to *Théorie d'ensemble*. As a result, Potter's film has been interpreted as an antitheoretical statement. What seems to be at issue, however, is the inadequacy of currently existing theoretical constructs to account for the specificity of a woman's experience. For as we are told, the heroine of the film is "searching for a theory that would explain her life and her death." On *Thriller*, see Jane Weinstock, "She Who Laughs First Laughs Last," *Camera Obscura*, 5 (1980).

20. Published in *Screen*, 16, 3 (Autumn 1975).
21. See my "Earthwords," *October*, 10 (Fall 1979), pp. 120-132.
22. "No Essential Femininity: A Conversation between Mary Kelly and Paul Smith," *Parachute*, 26 (Spring 1982), p. 33.
23. Lyotard, *La condition postmoderne*, p. 8.
24. Ibid., p. 68.
25. Jameson, "'In the Destructive Element Immerse': Hans-Jürgen Syberberg and Cultural Revolution," *October*, 17 (Summer 1981), p. 113.
26. See, for example, "Fantasia of the Library," in D.F. Bouchard, ed. *Language, counter-memory, practice* (Ithaca: Cornell University Press, 1977), pp. 87-109. See also Douglas Crimp, "On the Museum's Ruins," in the present volume.
27. See Jameson, "Postmodernism and Consumer Society," in the present volume.
28. Jameson, *Political Unconscious*, p. 19.
29. White, p. 3.
30. Thus, the antithesis to narrative may well be allegory, which Angus Fletcher identifies as the "epitome of counter-narrative." Condemned by modern aesthetics because it speaks of the inevitable reclamation of the works of man by nature, allegory is also the epitome of the antimodern, for it views history as an irreversible process of dissolution and decay. The melancholic, contemplative gaze of the allegorist need not, however, be a sign of defeat; it may represent the superior wisdom of one who has relinquished all claims to mastery.
31. Translated by William Lovitt and published in *The Question Concerning Technology* (New York: Harper and Row, 1977), pp. 115-54. I have, of course, oversimplified Heidegger's complex and, I believe, extremely important argument.
32. Ibid, p. 149, 50. Heidegger's definition of the modern age—as the age of representation for the purpose of mastery—coincides with Theodor Adorno and Max Horkheimer's treatment of modernity in their *Dialectic of Enlightenment* (written in exile in 1944, but without real impact until its republication in 1969). "What men want to learn from nature," Adorno and Horkheimer write, "is how to use it in order wholly to dominate it and other men." And the primary means of realizing this desire is (what Heidegger, at least, would recognize as) representation—the suppression of "the multitudinous affinities between existents" in favor of "the single relation between the subject who bestows meaning and the meaningless object." What seems even more significant, in the context of this essay, is that Adorno and Horkheimer repeatedly identify this operation as "patriarchal."
33. Jameson, "Interview," *diacritics*, 12, 3 (Fall 1982), p. 87.
34. Lyotard, *La condition postmoderne*, p. 63. Here, Lyotard argues that the *grands récits* of modernity contain the seeds of their own delegitimation.
35. For more on this group of painters, see my "Honor, Power and the Love of Women," *Art in America*, 71, 1 (January 1983), pp. 7-13.
36. Martha Rosler interviewed by Martha Gever in *Afterimage* (October 1981), p. 15. *The Bowery in Two Inadequate Descriptive Systems* has been published in Rosler's book *3 Works* (Halifax: The Press of The Nova Scotia College of Art and Design, 1981).
37. "Intellectuals and Power: A conversation between Michel Foucault and Gilles Deleuze," *Language, counter-memory, practice*, p. 209. Deleuze to Foucault: "In my opinion, you were the first—in your books and in the practical sphere—to teach us something absolutely fundamental: the indignity of speaking for others."
   The idea of a counter-discourse also derives from this conversation, specifically from Foucault's work with the "Groupe d'information de prisons." Thus, Foucault: "When the prisoners began to speak, they possessed an individual theory of prisons, the penal system, and justice. It is this form of discourse which ultimately matters, a discourse against

power, the counter-discourse of prisoners and those we call delinquents—and not a theory *about* delinquency."

38. Martha Rosler, "in, around, and afterthoughts (on documentary photography)," *3 Works,* p. 79.
39. Quoted in Heath, p. 84.
40. Interview with Luce Irigaray in M.-F. Hans and G. Lapouge, eds., *Les femmes, la pornographie, l'erotisme* (Paris, 1978), p. 50.
41. *Civilization and Its Discontents,* trans. J. Strachey (New York: Norton, 1962), pp. 46-7.
42. Jane Gallop, *Feminism and Psychoanalysis: The Daughter's Seduction* (Ithaca: Cornell University Press, 1982), p. 27.
43. "On Fetishism," repr. in Philip Rieff, ed., *Sexuality and the Psychology of Love* (New York: Collier, 1963), p. 217.
44. Lacan, p. 90.
45. On Barthes's refusal of mastery, see Paul Smith, "We Always Fail—Barthes' Last Writings," *SubStance,* 36 (1982), pp. 34-39. Smith is one of the few male critics to have directly engaged the feminist critique of patriarchy without attempting to rewrite it.
46. Benjamin Buchloh, "Allegorical Procedures: Appropriation and Montage in Contemporary Art," *Artforum,* XXI, 1 (September 1982), pp. 43-56.
47. Lacan's suggestion that "the phallus can play its role only when veiled" suggests a different inflection of the term "unveil"—one that is not, however, Buchloh's.
48. On Birnbaum's work, see my "Phantasmagoria of the Media," *Art in America,* 70, 5 (May 1982), pp. 98-100.
49. See Alice A. Jardine, "Theories of the Feminine: Kristeva," *enclitic,* 4, 2 (Fall 1980), pp. 5-15.
50. "The author is reputed the father and owner of his work: literary science therefore teaches *respect* for the manuscript and the author's declared intentions, while society asserts the legality of the relation of author to work (the *'droit d'auteur'* or 'copyright,' in fact of recent date since it was only really legalized at the time of the French Revolution). As for the Text, it reads without the inscription of the Father." Roland Barthes, "From Work to Text," *Image/Music/Text,* trans. S. Heath (New York: Hill and Wang, 1977), pp. 160-61.
51. Levine's first appropriations were images of maternity (women in their natural role) from ladies' magazines. She then took landscape photographs by Eliot Porter and Andreas Feininger, then Weston's portraits of Neil, then Walker Evans's FSA photographs. Her recent work is concerned with the involvement with images of alterity remains: she has exhibited reproductions of Franz Marc's pastoral depictions of animals, and Egon Schiele's self-portraits (madness). On the thematic consistency of Levine's "work," see my review, "Sherrie Levine at A & M Artworks," *Art in America,* 70, 6 (Summer 1982), p. 148.
52. See Metz, "The Imaginary Signifier."
53. Douglas Crimp, "Appropriating Appropriation," in Paula Marincola, ed., *Image Scavengers: Photography* (Philadelphia: Institute of Contemporary Art, 1982), p. 34.
54. Hélène Cixous, "Entretien avec Francoise van Rossum-Guyon," quoted in Heath, p. 96.
55. Sherman's shifting identity is reminiscent of the authorial strategies of Eugenie Lemoine-Luccioni as discussed by Jane Gallop, see *Feminism and Psychoanalysis,* p. 105: "Like children, the various productions of an author date from different moments, and cannot strictly be considered to have the same origin, the same author. At least we must avoid the fiction that a person is the same, unchanging throughout time. Lemoine-Luccioni makes the difficulty patent by signing each text with a different name, all of which are 'hers'."
56. See, for example, Martha Rosler's criticisms in "Notes on Quotes," p. 73: "Repeating the images of woman bound in the frame will, like Pop, soon be seen as a *confirmation* by the 'post-feminist' society."

57. Hal Foster, "Subversive Signs," *Art in America,* 70, 10 (November 1982), p. 88.
58. For a statement of this position in relation to contemporary artistic production, see Mario Perniola, "Time and Time Again," *Artforum,* XXI, 8 (April 1983); pp. 54-55. Perniola is indebted to Baudrillard; but are we not back with Ricoeur in 1962—that is, at precisely the point at which we started?

The Object of Post-Criticism

GREGORY L. ULMER

What is at stake in the controversy surrounding contemporary critical writing is easier to understand when placed in the context of modernism and postmodernism in the arts. The issue is "representation"—specifically, the representation of the object of study in a critical text. Criticism now is being transformed in the same way that literature and the arts were transformed by the avant-garde movements in the early decades of this century. The break with "mimesis," with the values and assumptions of "realism," which revolutionized the modernist arts, is now underway (belatedly) in criticism, the chief consequence of which, of course, is a change in the relation of the critical text to its object—literature.

A rationale for this shift may be found in Hayden White's complaint that "when historians claim that history is a combination of science and art, they generally mean that it is a combination of late-nineteenth-century social science and mid-nineteenth-century art," modelled on the novels of Scott or Thackeray.[1] White suggests, instead, that historians of literature (or of any discipline, for that matter) should use *contemporary* scientific and artistic insights and methods as the basis for their work, pursuing "the possibility of using impressionistic, expressionistic, surrealistic, and (perhaps) even actionist modes of representation for dramatizing the significance of data which they have uncovered but which all too frequently they are prohibited from seriously contemplating as evidence" (*Tropics,* pp. 42, 47-8). I will argue, following White's lead, that "post-criticism" (-modernist, -structuralist) is constituted precisely by the application of the devices of modernist art to critical representations; furthermore, that the principal device taken over by the critics and theorists is the compositional pair collage/montage.

83

Collage/Montage

By most accounts, collage is the single most revolutionary formal innovation in artistic representation to occur in our century.[2] Although the technique itself is ancient, collage was introduced into the "high arts" (as is well known) by Braque and Picasso as a solution to the problems raised by analytic cubism, a solution which finally provided an alternative to the "illusionism" of perspective which had dominated Western painting since the early Renaissance.

> In a still-life scene at a café, with lemon, oyster, glass, pipe, and newspaper [*Still-Life with Chair Caning* (1912), the first cubist collage], Picasso glued a piece of oilcloth on which is printed the pattern of woven caning, thus indicating the presence of a chair without the slightest use of traditional methods. For just as the painted letters JOU signify JOURNAL, a section of facsimile caning signifies the whole chair. Later Picasso would go one step further and incorporate into his collages actual objects or fragments of objects, signifying literally themselves. This strange idea was to transform cubism and to become the source for much of twentieth-century art.[3]

The interest of collage as a device for criticism resides partly in the objectivist impulse of cubism (as opposed to the non-objective movements which it inspired). The cubist collage, by incorporating directly into the work an actual fragment of the referent (open form), remains "representational" while breaking completely with the *trompe l'oeil* illusionism of traditional realism. Moreover, "these tangible and non-illusionistic objects presented a new and original source of interplay between artistic expressions and the experience of the everyday world. An unpredicted and significant step in bringing art and life closer to being a simultaneous experience had been taken."[4]

It is not necessary to repeat here the historical account of how collage became the predominate, all-pervasive device of 20th-century arts. Rather I will note the principles of collage/montage which have directed representations in a diversity of arts and media, including most recently literary criticism: "To lift a certain number of elements from works, objects, preexisting messages, and to integrate them in a new creation in order to produce an original totality manifesting ruptures of diverse sorts."[5] The operation, which may be recognized as a kind of "bricolage" (Lévi-Strauss), includes four characteristics — découpage (or severing); preformed or extant messages or materials; assemblage (montage); discontinuity or heterogeneity. "Collage" is the transfer of materials from one context to another, and "montage" is the "dissemination" of these borrowings through the new setting (*Collages,* 72). Two features of collage illustrated in *Still Life with Chair Caning* are worth noting here: 1) that the borrowed fragment is a signifier "that would summarize in one form many characteristics of a given object" (Fry, 32-3); 2) the chair caning is in fact represented by a *simulacrum*—the printed oil cloth—which is nevertheless a readymade addition rather than an illusionistic reproduction.

Photography is an equally useful model for the mode of representation adopted by post-criticism—if it is understood not as the culmination of linear perspective, but as a means of *mechanical reproduction* (as described in Walter Benjamin's famous article). The analogy between post-criticism and the revolution in representation which transformed the arts, then, should include as well the principle of photographic representation in both its realist and semiotic versions. Considered at this level of generalization, photographic representation may be described according to the collage principle. Indeed, it is a collage machine (perfected in television), producing simulacra of the life-world: 1) Photography selects and transfers a fragment of the visual continuum into a new frame. The realist argument, most forcefully stated by André Bazin, is that because of mechanical reproduction, which forms the image of the world automatically without the intervention of human "creativity" (the reduction of this "creativity" to the act of selection, as in the readymade), "the photographic image is a kind of decal or transfer, . . . [it] is the object itself." [6] 2) Although semiotics prefers to designate this relation to the real in terms of iconic and indexical signifiers, the photographic image signifies itself and something else—it becomes a signifier remotivated within the system of a new frame. There are several versions of the argument that photography (or film) is a language, best summarized in Sergei Eisenstein's notion of "intellectual montage," in which the real is used as an element of a discourse.

The strongest version of the semiotic theory of photography is realized in the strategies of photomontage (in which are joined, in any case, the principles of photography and collage/montage). In photomontage the photographic images are themselves cut out and pasted into new, surprising, provoking juxtapositions, as in John Heartfield's *The Meaning of the Hitlerian Salute* (1933), which, besides the title, consists of:

> A caption which takes the form of one of Hitler's slogans: "I have millions behind me." An image: in right profile Hitler gives the Hitlerian salute, but reversed to the back [his unique version of the gesture, with palm flipped back, fingers extended beside his ear]. His silhouette reaches only to the middle of the image. Above his palm [is] a wad of banknotes being handed to him by a large-bellied figure, dressed in black, immense and anonymous (one barely sees his chin).[7]

Hitler's words as well as his image are turned against him in this recombination, revealing in a stroke the link between German capitalism and the Nazi party.

Photomontage illustrates the "productive" potential of collage promoted by Walter Benjamin and Bertolt Brecht (among others). "I am speaking of the procedure of montage: the superimposed element disrupts the context in which it is inserted," Benjamin says, describing Brecht's plays. "The interruption of action, on account of which Brecht described his theatre as *epic*, constantly counteracts an illusion in the audience. For such illusion is a hindrance to a theater that proposes to make use of elements of reality in experimental rearrangements.... [The spectator] recognizes it as the real situation, not with satisfaction, as in the theatre of naturalism, but with astonishment. Epic theatre, therefore, does not reproduce situations, rather it discovers them." [8]

Brecht defended the mechanics of collage/montage against Georg Lukács's socialist realism (based on the aesthetics of 19th-century fiction) as an alternative to the organic model of growth and its classic assumptions of harmony, unity, linearity, closure. Montage does not reproduce the real, but constructs an object (its lexical field includes the terms "assemble, build, join, unite, add, combine, link, construct, organize"—*Montage*, 121) or rather, mounts a process ("the relation of form to content is no longer a relation of exteriority, the form resembling clothes which can dress no matter what content, it is *process, genesis, result of a work*"—*Montage*, 120) in order to intervene in the world, not to reflect but to change reality.

There is nothing innately subversive about the photomontage principle, or any other formal device. Rather, as we are often reminded, such effects must be continually reinvented. Part of the interest of this context for post-criticism is that the debates among Lukács, Brecht, Benjamin, Adorno, et al with respect to the value of montage experiments in literature will no doubt be reiterated now with respect to criticism. Will the collage/montage revolution in representation be admitted into the academic essay, into the discourse of knowledge, replacing the "realist" criticism based on the notions of "truth" as correspondence to or correct reproduction of a referent object of study? The question of post-criticism was first posed in just this way by Roland Barthes in his reply to the attack made on his Racine book by Raymond Picard (who associated Barthes with dadaism). Barthes explained that the modernist poets, beginning at least with Mallarmé, had demonstrated already the unification of poetry and criticism—that literature was itself a critique of language, and that criticism had no "meta"-language capable of describing or accounting for literature. Barthes concluded that the categories of literature and criticism could no longer be kept apart, that now there were only *writers*. The relation of the critical text to its object of study was to be conceived in terms no longer of subject-object but of subject-predicate (authors and critics both facing the same material—language), with critical "meaning" being a "simulacrum" of the literary text, a new "flowering" of the rhetoric at work in literature. The critic's text, he says, suggesting the systematic transformation relating the two writings, is an *anamorphosis* of its object—an analogy with distorted perspective which, in post-criticism, is joined by the analogy with collage/montage.[9]

The response to his "paraliterary"[10] initiative was violent and hostile, Barthes explained, because his project, following the lead of the artists themselves, touched language directly.[11] Jacques Derrida recently restated this criterion of critical vanguardism: "The deconstruction of a pedagogical institution and all that it implies. What this institution cannot bear, is for anyone to tamper with language.... It can bear more readily the most apparently revolutionary ideological sorts of 'content,' if only that content does not touch the borders of language and of all the juridico-political contracts that it guarantees."[12]

Grammatology

That Jacques Derrida should explore the lessons of the modernist revolution in representation is understandable, considering that he undertakes a deconstruction of the very concept and philosophy of mimesis. "Mimesis," which Derrida labels "mimetologism," refers to that capture of representation by the metaphysics of "logocentrism," the era extending from Plato to Freud (and beyond) in which writing (all manner of inscription) is reduced to a secondary status as "vehicle," in which the signified or referent is always *prior* to the material sign, the purely intelligible prior to the merely sensible.[13] "It is not a question of 'rejecting' these notions," Derrida writes. "They are necessary and, at least at present, nothing is conceivable for us without them.... Since these concepts are indispensable for unsettling the heritage to which they belong, we should be even less prone to renounce them" (*Grammatology*, 14-15). Derrida's alternative to "mimetologism," then, does *not* abandon or deny reference, but re-thinks reference in another way: "It complicates the boundary line that ought to run between the text and what seems to lie beyond its fringes, what is classed as the *real*."[14]

It is becoming apparent that in his reliance on collage/montage as the stylistic device with which to deconstruct mimesis, Derrida is doing for this new mode of representation what Aristotle, in the *Poetics*, did for "mimetologism." In the same way that Aristotle provided at once a theory of tragedy (mimesis) and a method (formal analysis) for the study of all literary modes, Derrida in a text such as *Glas* (identified as the "exemplary" text of poststructuralism[15]) provides a "theory" of montage (grammatology) and a method (deconstruction) for working with any mode of writing whatsoever. Derrida is the "Aristotle" of montage.

In spite of its associated complexities and controversies, Derrida's basic formulation of the nature of language is relatively simple, a formulation which, placed in the context of the collage paradigm, takes on its fullest significance. Grammatology is "poststructuralist" in that it replaces the "sign" (composed of signifier and signified—the most basic unit of meaning according to structuralism) with a still more basic unit—the *gram*.

> It is a question of producing a new concept of writing. This concept can be called *gram* or *différance*. . . . Whether in the order of spoken or written discourse, no element can function as a sign without referring to another element which itself is not simply present. This interweaving results in each 'element'—phoneme or grapheme—being constituted on the basis of the trace within it of the other elements of the chain or system. This interweaving, this textile, is the *text* produced only in the transformation of another text. Nothing, neither among the elements nor within the system, is anywhere ever simply present or absent. There are only, everywhere, differences and traces of traces. The gram, then, is the most general concept of semiology—which thus becomes grammatology.[16]

Collage/montage, in other words, is the manifestation at the level of discourse of the "gram" principle, as will be made clear when its definition is compared with the following rhetorical definition of the collage effect:

> Its [collage's] heterogeneity, even if it is reduced by every operation of composition, imposes itself on the reading as stimulation to produce a signification which could be neither univocal nor stable. Each cited element breaks the continuity or the linearity of the discourse and leads necessarily to a double reading: that of the fragment perceived in relation to its text of origin; that of the same fragment as incorporated into a new whole, a different totality. The trick of collage consists also of never entirely suppressing the alterity of these elements reunited in a temporary composition. Thus the art of collage proves to be one of the most effective strategies in the putting into question of all the illusions of representation (*Collages,* 34-5).

This undecidable reading effect, oscillating between presence and absence, is just what Derrida tries to achieve at every level of his "double science," from his paleonymic redefinition (remotivation) of concepts to his publishing of two books under one cover (*Glas*).

The notion of the gram is especially useful for theorizing the evident fact, much discussed in structuralist psychoanalysis (Lacan) and ideological criticism (Althusser), that signifieds and signifiers are continually breaking apart and reattaching in new combinations, thus revealing the inadequacy of Saussure's model of the sign, according to which the signifier and the signified relate as if they were two sides of the same sheet of paper. The tendency of Western philosophy throughout its history ("logocentrism") to try to pin down and fix a specific signified to a given signifier violates, according to grammatology, the nature of language, which functions not in terms of matched *pairs* (signifier/signifieds) but of *couplers* or *couplings* — "a person or thing that couples or links together." The following description of what Derrida calls "iterability" is also an excellent summary of the collage consequences of the gram:

> And this is the possibility on which I want to insist: the possibility of dis-engagement and citational graft which belongs to the structure of every mark, spoken or written, and which constitutes every mark in writing before and outside of every horizon of semio-linguistic communication; in writing, which is to say in the possibility of its functioning being cut off, at a certain point, from its 'original' desire-to-say-what-one-means and from its participation in a saturable and constraining context. Every sign, linguistic or non-linguistic, spoken or written (in the current sense of this opposition), in a small or large unit, can be *cited,* put between quotation marks; in so doing it can break with every given context, engendering an infinity of new contexts in a manner which is absolutely illimitable.[17]

In criticism, as in literature, collage takes the form of citation, but citation carried to an extreme (in post-criticism), collage being the "limit-case" of citation, and grammatology being the theory of writing as citation (cf. *Collages,* 301).

A useful point of departure for reviewing Derrida's own montage practice is the collection entitled *Dissemination* (a term which is listed as a synonym for collage/montage—*Collages,* 23) of which he says that "the most general title of the problem treated in those texts would be: castration and mimesis" (*Positions,* 84). In citing the object of study or in offering examples as illustrations, the critic is in the position of castrator: "Such a decision is a castration, at least acted out or feigned, or a circumcision. This is as it always is, and the knife that with obsessive frequency slashes the tree of *Numbers* [the text Derrida "studies" in the essay "Dissemination"] hones itself as a phallic threat. . . . The 'operation' of reading/writing goes by the way of *'the blade of a red knife' "* (*Dissemination,* 301). But rather than elaborating this connection between writing and psychoanalysis (exploited at length in Derrida's texts), I will confine myself to noting the two chief elements of Derrida's post-critical technique—grafting and mimicry:

1. *Graft.* Derrida's discussion of montage writing as "grafting" in "Dis-semination" is itself couched in the collage style (it *does* what it *says*), in a text consisting of nearly equal portions of selections from *Numbers* (a French "new new novel" by Philippe Sollers) and Derrida's frame text. "To write," Derrida states, "means to graft. It's the same word" (*Dis-semination,* 355). Then, in a description of method which applies as much to his own as to Sollers's writing, he adds, distinguishing post-critical from conventional collage:

Hence all those textual samples provided by *Numbers* do not, as you might have been tempted to believe, serve as "quotations," "collages," or even "illustrations." They are not being applied upon the surface or in the interstices of a text that would already exist without them. And they themselves can only be read within the operation of their reinscription, within the graft. It is the sustained, discrete violence of an incision that is not apparent in the thickness of the text, a calculated insemination of the proliferating allogene through which the two texts are transformed, deform each other, contaminate each other's content, tend at times to reject each other, or pass elliptically one into the other and become regenerated in the repetition, along the edges of an *overcast seam*. Each grafted text continues to radiate back toward the site of its removal, transforming that too, as it affects the new territory (*Dissemination,* 355).[18]

The new representation, the new status of the example mounted in the critical frame, has to do in part with the shift away from commentary and explanation, which rely on concepts, to work instead by means of examples—both in terms of the substitution of examples for arguments in one's own writing,[19] and of approaching the object of study (when it is another critical or theoretical text) at the level of the examples it uses.[20] "Clip out an example, since you cannot and should not undertake the infinite commentary that at every moment seems necessarily to engage and immediately to annul itself" (*Dissemination,* 300). If the clipping is associated with "castration" ("So make some incision, some violent arbitrary cut"), the montage or dissemination of the fragments thus collected in the new frame is associated with "invagination" (collage/montage is a bisexual writing).

The logic of examples governed by the principle of invagination is itself illustrated by the "loop hole" of a figure borrowed from set theory (the modern heir of the notion of the "concept" as a "having" or "belonging to") in order to describe the paradoxical escape of the "example" from conceptualization (collage writing being a kind of theft which violates "property" in every sense—intellectual property protected by copyright, and the properties of a given concept). The illustration figures that which Derrida formulates as the "law of the law of genre":

It is precisely a principle of contamination, a law of impurity, a parasitical economy. In the code of set theories, if I may use it at least figuratively, I would speak of a sort of participation without belonging—a taking part in without being part of, without having membership in a set. The trait that marks membership inevitably divides, the boundary of the set comes to form, by invagination, an internal pocket larger than the whole; and the outcome of this division and of this abounding remains as singular as it is limitless.[21]

Derrida's strategy with regard to "invagination" (matting or mounting the example) is to find a mode of critical "mimesis" which, like the law of the law of genre, would relate to its objects of study as an excess (and vice-versa)—the "law of participation without membership, of contamination," similar to the paradox of the hierarchy of classification in set theory: "The re-mark of belonging does not belong" ("Genre," 212).

The question Derrida poses, faced with the problem of comparing Blanchot's *L'arrêt de mort* with Shelley's *The Triumph of Life,* but seeking an alternative to "mimetological" commentary, is: "How can one text, assuming its unity, give or present another to be read, without touching it, without saying anything about it, practically without referring to it?" ("Borderlines," 80). His solution is to "endeavor to create an effect of *superimposing,* of superimprinting one text on the other," the text as "palimpsest" or "macula," a double band or "double bind" procedure which breaks with the conventional assumptions of criticism and pedagogy: "One procession is superimposed on the other, accompanying it without accompanying it." But, "You can't give a course on Shelley without ever mentioning him, pretending to deal with Blanchot, and more than a few others" ("Borderlines," 83-4). One version of the solution, utilized in "Dissemination" and *Glas,* is simply to interpolate rhythmically (the "art of interruption" as a kind of music) a series of citations from the "host" texts. But, as *Glas* proves, citation produces excessively long texts. The model for a writing which goes beyond juxtaposition to superimposition is not collage but photography. "Borderlines" itself is compared (with respect to the problem of translation) to a "film for developing," for "processing" —hence, the text as "procession." "This superimposing is readable," Derrida adds, referring to a double-exposed print in Blanchot's story, "on a 'photograph'" ("Borderlines," 77, 85). The task of post-criticism, in other words, is to think the consequences for critical representation of the new mechanical means of reproduction (film and magnetic tape—technologies which require collage/montage composition) in the way that Brecht, as Benjamin noted in "The Author as Producer," had done for theatrical representation. Derrida formulates his new mimesis of superimposition in terms of mime.

2. *Mime.* The most important innovation in Derrida's practice of montage is a "new mimesis" in which the text mimes its object of study.[22] *Dissemination* turns out to be a unified study in that the theory of a new mimesis worked out in the first two essays ("Plato's Pharmacy" is a review of "mimesis" in Platonic philosophy; "The Double Session" is a review of Mallarmé's alternative to Platonic mimesis, discovered in mime) is applied in the concluding piece ("Dissemination"). The chief lesson of "Plato's Pharmacy" is that any composition which works according to the principle

of mechanical reproduction falls under the category (despised in Platonic philosophy) of hypomnesis or artificial memory; hypomnesis can only mime knowledge. The sophist sells only "the signs and insignia of science; not memory itself (*mneme*), only monuments (*hypomnemata*), inventories, archives, citations, copies, accounts, tales, lists, notes, duplicates, chronicles, genealogies, references. Not memory but memorials" (*Dissemination*, 106-7). Writing, in short, is a simulacrum of "true science." But "true science," from Plato to positivism, is what post-criticism puts in question.

> We are today on the eve of Platonism. Which can also, naturally, be thought of as the morning after Hegelianism. At that specific point, the *philosophia*, the *episteme* are not "overturned," "rejected," "reined in," etc., in the name of something like writing; quite the contrary. But they are, according to a relation that philosophy would call *simulacrum*, according to a more subtle excess of truth, assumed and at the same time displaced into a completely different field, where one can still, but that's all, "mime absolute knowledge" (*Dissemination*, 107-8).

Secondly, Derrida concludes from his extensive analysis of Mallarmé's *Mimique* (in "The Double Session") that mime models an alternative to Platonic mimesis.

> We are faced then with mimicry imitating nothing.... There is no simple reference. It is in this that the mime's operation does allude, but alludes to nothing.... Mallarmé thus preserves the differential structure of mimicry or *mimesis*, but without its Platonic or metaphysical interpretation, which implies that somewhere the being of something that *is*, is being imitated. Mallarmé even maintains (and maintains himself in) the structure of the *phantasma* as it is defined by Plato: the simulacrum as the copy of a copy. With the exception that there is no longer any model, and hence no copy (*Dissemination*, 206).

Once one realizes that the mime emblematizes (for Derrida) mechanical reproduction, it becomes apparent that representation without reference is a description of the way film or tape functions as a "language," receiving exact copies of sights and sounds (in collage terms, mechanical reproduction removes or lifts sights and sounds from their contexts—*de*-motivates them, hence the *loss* of reference, the undecidability of allusion), only to *re*-motivate them as signifiers in a new system. Mallarmé earns the label of "modernist" by detaching mimicry from logocentric mimetology; Derrida becomes "postmodernist" by putting mimicry to work in the interest of a new reference (discussed as "allegory" in the next section).

Derrida's first experiments with mimed writing consisted largely of the collage procedure of direct, massive citation ("Here again I do nothing more, can do nothing more than cite, as you will come perhaps to see," [*Glas*, 24]). The working assumption was that repetition is "originary"—

"Repeated, the same line is no longer exactly the same, the ring no longer has the same center, *the origin has played.*" [23] Derrida's desire to superimpose one text on the other (the program to which mimicry is addressed) is an attempt to devise a system of reference or representation which works in terms of *différance*, [24] with its reversible temporality, rather than in terms of the irreversible time of the sign. From the very beginning, then, the strategy of deconstruction has been repetition: "There is probably no choice to be made between two lines of thought; our task is rather to reflect on the circularity which makes the one pass into the other indefinitely. And, by strictly repeating this *circle* in its own historical possibility, we allow the production of some *elliptical* change of site, within the difference involved in repetition." [25] Here we have the earliest version of text as "texture"—"touching" language—in which the deconstructive writing *traces* the surface of the object of study (writing as "tracing") looking for "flaws" or "faults"—the openings of joints, articulations, where the text might be dismembered. The deconstruction is accomplished in fact by borrowing the very terms utilized by the host work itself—"difference" from Saussure, "supplement" from Rousseau, and so on—and remotivating them, detaching them (following the principle of the gram) from one conceptual set or semantic field and reattaching them to another (but always with the most systematic attention to the potentials or materials available in the word itself).

As the strategy of "literal" repetition developed, the borrowing of terms and the direct citations were supplemented with the construction of general simulacra of the object of study. The practice is clearly illustrated in an extreme case, such as "Cartouches" (in *La Vérité en Peinture*), in which the task is to mime in discourse a *visual* work. The referent is a work by Gérard Titus-Carmel entitled *The Pocket-Size Tlingit Coffin* (1975-76), consisting of a "sculpture"—a mahogany box of "modest" dimensions—and 127 drawings of this "model," each from a different angle. The relationship that exists within the *Tlingit Coffin* between the sculpture and the drawings emblematizes or remarks the relationship of Derrida's critical mimicry to its chosen referent ("model"). The sculpture (the box as model) "does not belong to the line of which it makes a part," but is heterogeneous to it (*Vérité*, 217). Derrida's own discourse, as noted earlier, "touches nothing," leaves the reader or viewer alone with the work, "passes beside it in silence, as another theory, another series, saying nothing about what it represents for me, nor even for him" (*Vérité*, 227).

Unlike Heidegger, who declared that art "speaks," Derrida insists on the muteness of the series, or on its capacity to work without concept, without conclusions: "Such would be the de-monstration. Let us not abuse the easy word-play. De-monstration proves without showing, without evidencing any conclusion, without entailing anything, without an available thesis. It proves according to a different mode, but proceeding with its step of demonstration [*pas de demonstration*] or non-demonstration. It transforms, it transforms itself, in its process rather than advancing a signifiable object of discourse." [26] The series of drawings, that is, de-monstrates the problem of order and representation in the relation of examples to models, which is why Derrida selected it, mounted it. Indeed, his own text relates to this referent the way the drawings relate to the box, an example mounted because, like *Numbers,* it exposes exposition.

The strategy for miming the *Tlingit Coffin* is to ignore the plastic objects as such (in the way that the "content" of *Numbers* essentially was ignored) and to mime the structuring process of the work—to concentrate on the generation of a "contingent" of terms (cartouche, paradigm, article, duction, contingent and the like) which are processed in a way parallel to the way Titus-Carmel runs through 127 variations in his drawings of the model, "putting them in perspective, turning them about in every sense (direction) by a series of swerves [*écarts*], variations, modulations, anamorphoses," finally stopping after a predetermined number of pages, creating the same effect of contingent necessity or arbitrary motivation as the series of exactly 127 drawings (*Vérité,* 229). The anagram and the homonym operate on the lexicon the way anamorphoses operate on representational perspective. Derrida mimes the dated drawings further by composing as if in a journal, with dated entries, each entry constituting a variation on a theme. Such is the logic of the simulacrum as translation, as verbal mimicry of a visual scene—a mimicry which functions similarly in other texts, regardless of referent.

The implication of textual mime for post-criticism, informing paraliterature as a hybrid of literature and criticism, art and science, is that knowledge of an object of study may be obtained without conceptualization or explanation. Rather, as if following Wittgenstein's admonition that "the meaning is the use," Derrida enacts or performs (mimes) the compositional structuration of the referent, resulting in another text of the same "kind" (genre—but "different" according to the "law of the law of genre" noted above). Post-criticism, then, functions with an "epistemology" of performance—knowing as making, producing, doing, acting, as in Wittgenstein's account of the relation of knowing to the "mastery of a technique." Thus post-criticism writes "on" its object in the way that Wittgenstein's knower exclaims, "Now I know how to go on!" [27]—with this "on" carrying all the dimensions and ambiguities of the "on" in Derrida's "Living On" (beyond, about, upon, on—including the parasitical connotation). Writing may show more (and other) than it says—the "surplus value" of writing which interests Derrida. The name of this "more" is "allegory."

Allegory

The importance of allegory for postmodernism has already been discussed by critics such as Craig Owens (among others) who in fact uses the writings of Derrida and Paul de Man to define the question. Owens identifies allegory with Derrida's notion of "supplement" (one of the many names Derrida assigns to the effect of the gram): "If allegory is identified as a supplement ["an expression externally added to another expression," hence "extra," yet supplying a lack], then it is also aligned with writing, insofar as writing is conceived as supplementary to speech."[28] Owens also makes good use of Derrida's notion of "deconstruction" to suggest how postmodernism goes "beyond formalism":

> The deconstructive impulse is characteristic of postmodernist art in general and must be distinguished from the self-critical tendency of modernism. Modernist theory presupposes that mimesis, the adequation of an image to a referent, can be bracketed or suspended, and that the art object itself can be substituted (metaphorically) for its referent.... Postmodernism neither brackets nor suspends the referent but works instead to problematize the activity of reference.[29]

Objections have been raised concerning the possibility of sustaining this distinction between self-reference and a problematized reference—both to Owen's statement and to Derrida's project.[30] These doubts about the "post," about the possibility of working "beyond" modernism or structuralism, are based in thought which is still semiological rather than grammatological. Grammatology has emerged on the far side of the formalist crisis and developed a discourse which is fully referential, but referential in the manner of "narrative allegory" rather than of "allegoresis." "Allegoresis," the mode of commentary long practiced by traditional critics, "suspends" the surface of the text, applying a terminology of "verticalness, levels, hidden meaning, the hieratic difficulty of interpretation," whereas "narrative allegory" (practiced by post-critics) explores the literal — *letteral* — level of the language itself, in a horizontal investigation of the polysemous meanings simultaneously available in the words themselves — in etymologies and puns — and in the things the words name. The allegorical narrative unfolds as a dramatization or enactment (personification) of the "literal truth inherent in the words themselves."[31] In short, narrative allegory favors the material of the signifier over the meanings of the signifieds.

An idea of how this material reference functions may be derived from the examples Owens mentions, including his point (supporting my discussion of photography) that film is the "primary vehicle for modern allegory" because of its mode of representation: "Film composes narrative out of a succession of concrete images, which makes it particularly suited to allegory's essential pictogrammatism"; and, citing Barthes, "'an allegory is a rebus, writing composed of concrete images'" ("Allegorical Impulse, Part 2," 74). Owens also cites the example of Sherrie Levine, who literally "takes" (other people's) photographs, as an extreme version of the allegorical capacity of collage as "readymade." The point of a recent allegorical project by Levine, in which she "selected, mounted, and framed Andreas Feininger's photographs of natural subjects," Owens explains, is the deconstruction of the opposition between nature and culture. "When Levine wants an image of nature, she does not produce one herself but appropriates another image, and this she does in order to expose the degree to which 'nature' is always already implicated in a system of cultural values which assigns it a specific, culturally determined position." [32] Levine, that is, de-monstrates the grammatological writing appropriate to the age of mechanical reproduction in which "copyright" now means the right to copy anything, a mimicry or repetition which is originary, producing differences (just as in allegory anything may mean anything else).

Post-critics write with the discourse of others (the already-written) the way Levine "takes" photographs. In the words of the great montage-ist of electronic music, John Cage, "with magnetic tape, the possibility exists to use the literature of music as material (cutting it up, transforming it, etc.); this is the best thing that could have happened to it." [33] Roland Barthes typifies the relationship between science and art which exists in para-literature. In this new "intellectual art," he explains, "we produce simultaneously theory, critical combat, and pleasure; we subject the objects of knowledge and discussion—as in any art—no longer to an instance of truth, but to a consideration of *effects*." [34] The point is that "one plays a science, one puts it in the picture—*like a piece in a collage*" (*Barthes*, 100). In his own case, Barthes often played with linguistics: "you use a pseudo-linguistics, a metaphorical linguistics: not that grammatical concepts seek out images in order to express themselves, but just the contrary, *because these concepts come to constitute allegories,* a second language, whose abstraction is diverted to fictive ends" (*Barthes,* 124). Barthes's statement is as precise a definition as it is possible to give of what post-criticism is, and of the way Derrida writes with, allegorizes, the gram.

Walter Benjamin, to whom Owens also alludes, is perhaps the principal precursor of the post-critical use of collage-allegory.

> Benjamin saw affinity between the allegoric imagination of the German baroque dramatists and the artistic needs of the twentieth century; first in the melancholy spirit of the former, with its emblematic but inscrutable insignia, which he rediscovered in Kafka; then in the cognate principle of montage

which he found in the work of Eisenstein and Brecht. Montage became for him the modern, constructive, active, unmelancholy form of allegory, namely the ability to connect dissimilars in such a way as to "shock" people into new recognitions and understandings.[35]

Benjamin applied the collage/montage style in the early *One-Way Street* (the cover of which, when it was published in 1928, displayed a photomontage by Sascha Stone as an icon of the technique applied in the text[36]). Defining the conventional academic book as "an outdated mediation between two different filing systems," [37] Benjamin wanted to write a book made up entirely of quotations in order to purge all subjectivity and allow the self to be a vehicle for the expression of "objective cultural tendencies" [38] (similar to Barthes's project in *A Lover's Discourse: Fragments*).

Benjamin's response to the problem of representation raised in philosophy by the modernist crisis was to abandon the conventional book form in favor of the essay—incomplete, digressive, without proof or conclusion, in which could be juxtaposed fragments, minute details ("close-ups") drawn from every level of the contemporary world. These details, of course, functioned allegorically. But there is an all-important difference between montage-allegory and the object as emblem in baroque and romantic allegory. In the latter, adhering to the model of the hieroglyph in which the particular object of nature or daily life is taken over as a conventional sign for an idea, the object is used "not to convey its natural characteristics, but those which we have ourselves lent it." [39] In collage, on the other hand, the allegorical significance is literal, derives from the natural characteristics themselves. "The 'truth' which Benjamin had discovered in this literary form [*Trauerspiel*], one which had been lost in the history of its interpretation, was that allegory was not an arbitrary representation of the idea which it portrayed. It was instead the concrete expression of that idea's material foundation." [40]

The style of the essay was to be an "art of interruption": "Interruption is one of the fundamental methods of all form-giving. It reaches far beyond the domain of art. It is, to mention just one of its aspects, the origin of the quotation" (*Brecht*, 19). Benjamin's procedure was "to collect and reproduce in quotation the contradictions of the present without resolution" —"the dialectic at a standstill," juxtaposing the extremes of a given idea. This collage strategy was itself an image of the "break-up," the "disintegration" of civilization in the modern world, relevant to one of Benjamin's most famous formulas: "Allegories are, in the realm of thoughts, what ruins are in the realm of things" (*Tragic Drama*, 178), the premise being that something becomes an object of knowledge only as it "decays," or is made to disintegrate (analysis as decay).

Theodor Adorno shares many of Benjamin's most basic assumptions about the value of the montage-allegory strategy. Adorno's method was derived in part from his studies with Arnold Schönberg. Adorno wanted to do to philosophical idealism what Schönberg, with his twelve-tone compositional procedure, had done to tonality in music. "Schönberg rejected the notion of artist-as-genius and replaced it with the artist as craftsman; he saw music not as the expression of subjectivity, but as a search for knowledge which lay outside the artist, as potential within the object, the material. For him, composing was discovery and invention through the practice of music-making" (Buck-Morss, 123). The method is objective because the "object" leads, criticism being a translation into words of the *inner logic of the object,* thing, event, text itself. Once articulated, however, the material could be "rearranged" in order to render intelligible its "truth":

> The thinker reflected on a sensuous and non-identical reality not in order to dominate it, not to butcher it to fit the Procrustean beds of mental categories or to liquidate its particularity by making it disappear under abstract concepts. Instead the thinker, like the artist, proceeded mimetically, and in the process of imitating matter transformed it so that it could be read as a monadological expression of social truth. In such philosophy, as in artworks, form was not indifferent to content—hence the central significance of representation, the manner of philosophical expression. Aesthetic creation itself was not subjective invention so much as the objective discovery of the new within the given, immanently, through a regrouping of its elements (Buck-Morss, 132).

Benjamin perhaps put this attitude most concisely when he cited Goethe's notion of the symbol as suggestive of how photographs "mean": "There is a sensitive empiricism which makes itself most inwardly identical with the object and thereby becomes genuine theory." [41] But it is important to realize that this object-become-theory in montage-allegory functions in terms of a representation which is neither allegorical nor symbolic in the traditional senses (the meanings are neither purely unmotivated nor motivated—the opposition deconstructed by grammatology, according to which "meaning" is a continual process of demotivation and remotivation). An important aspect of this "philosophy of the concrete particular," whose true interest is "with the nonconceptual, the singular and the particular; with that which since Plato has been dismissed as transitory and insignificant, and upon which Hegel hung the label of 'foul existence,'" (Buck-Morss, 69), first intuited by Benjamin and then formalized by Adorno, is its ability to exploit the tension between science and art in a way that anticipates the strategy of post-criticism. Indeed, Adorno's description of the method as "exact fantasy" ("fantasy which abides strictly within the material which the sciences present to it, and reaches beyond them only in the smallest aspects of their arrangement: aspects, granted, which fantasy itself must originally generate" [Buck-Morss, 86]) outlines the project of poststructuralist theory—to locate the "subject" of knowledge—and of "pragmatics"—to study the user's (knower's) attitude to the message.

What the baroque or romantic allegorist conceived of as an emblem, the post-critic treats as a model. A good example of Derrida's use of the quotidian object as a theoretical model is found in *Spurs, Nietzsche's Styles*. *Spurs* is a divagation on a fragment found in Nietzsche's Notebooks—"I have forgotten my umbrella"—apparently a meaningless citation, randomly noted. Derrida performs an "exact fantasy" apropos of this fragment, whose undecidable status, he argues, is replicated in Nietzsche's complete works (and in Derrida's own oeuvre as well). In the process of making this point, Derrida appropriates the umbrella as an icon marking or modelling the very structure of style as such: "The style-spur, the spurring style, is a long object, an oblong object, a word, which perforates even as it parries. It is the oblongi-foliated point (a spur or a spar) which derives its apotropaic power from the taut, resistant tissues, webs, sails and veils which are erected, furled and unfurled around it. But, it must not be forgotten, it is also an umbrella." [42]

The "double" structure of style—relevant to the problem of allegorical representation which at once reveals and conceals—finds, in the "morphology" of the umbrella with its shaft and fabric, a concrete model. Derrida borrows the "umbrella" left behind in Nietzsche's Notebooks and remotivates it (its meaning was indeterminate in any case) as a de-monstrative device. The umbrella counts for Derrida not as a "symbol," Freudian or otherwise, not as a meaning at all, but as a structural machine which, in its capacity to open and close, de-monstrates the unrepresentable gram.

A review of Derrida's texts turns up a small collection of such borrowed theoretical objects, including, besides the umbrella, a pair of shoes (from Van Gogh),[13] a fan (from Mallarmé), a matchbox (from Genet), a post card (from Freud)—all displaying the double structure of the gram. Together they constitute a collage, to be entitled "Still Life" (as models of writing they necessarily manifest the death drive); or perhaps "Autoportrait," in the surrealist mode, since each of these objects occurs in a discussion of fetishism. Let it suffice to say that the "example" in post-criticism functions in the manner of a "fetish object," thus linking allegory with psychoanalysis in paraliterature.

Parasite/Saprophyte

A model for the relation of the post-critical text to its object of study, often mentioned in the debate between traditional and post-critics, is that of parasite to host. J. Hillis Miller, speaking for the deconstructionists in a conference session on "The Limits of Pluralism," offered a rebuttal of

Wayne Booth's assertion (seconded by M.H. Abrams) that the "deconstruc-tionist reading of a given work is plainly and simply parasitical on the obvious or univocal reading." [44] Given that Derrida describes grammatology as a "parasitical economy," this term may not be as "wounding" as Booth and Abrams intend. Miller's response is to problematize the meaning of "parasite": "What happens when a critical essay extracts a 'passage' and 'cites' it? Is this different from a citation, echo, or allusion within a poem? Is a citation an alien parasite within the body of its host, the main text, or is it the other way around, the interpretative text the parasite which surrounds and strangles the citation which is its host?" The issue is compounded in the case of post-criticism, which carries citation to its limit—collage.

Miller's rebuttal is meant to undermine the very notion of "univocal" reading by showing the equivocal, paradoxical plurality of the meaning of "host" and "guest," which turn out to share the same etymological root and are interchangeable in their sense. The point of this etymological exercise, he says,

> is an argument for the value of recognizing the great complexity and equivocal richness of apparently obvious or univocal language, even the language of criticism, which is in this respect continuous with the language of literature. This complexity and equivocal richness resides in part in the fact that there is no conceptual expression without figure, and no intertwining of concept and figure without an implied story, narrative, or myth, in this case the story of the alien guest in the home. Deconstruction is an investigation of what is implied by this inherence of figure, concept, and narrative in one another (Miller, 443).

In short, Miller's definition of "deconstruction" is what Maureen Quilligan describes as the operation of narrative allegory.

It so happens that Michel Serres has provided a full elaboration—allegory—of the very story of deconstruction, of the alien guest in the home, in a paraliterary text entitled *Parasite*. Not only does Serres support Miller's point regarding the equivocality of the host-parasite terminology, he supplements it by noting that in French a third meaning is available which permits the story of the parasite to be explored literally as an allegory of communication theory (or rather, as with the gram, the theory itself pro-duces the allegory):

> The parasite is a microbe, an insidious infection that takes without giving and weakens without killing. The parasite is also a guest, who exchanges his talk, praise, and flattery for food. The parasite is noise as well, the static in a system or the interference in a channel. These seemingly dissimilar activities are, according to Michel Serres, not merely coincidentally expressed by the same word (in French). Rather, they are intrinsically related and, in fact, they have the same basic function in a system. Whether it produces a fever or just hot air, the parasite is a thermal exciter. And as such, it is both the atom of a relation and the production of a change in this relation. [45]

Taking the luck of this homonym as a clue, Serres researches a selection of literary examples, stories about dinners, hosts and guests, beginning with the fables of La Fontaine and including the return of Odysseus among the suitors, the *Symposium, Tartuffe,* etc., all examined in terms of *interruption,* interference, the noise which frightens away the mice, the call which took Simonides away from the table just before the roof collapsed (his recollection of which guest was sitting where, for purposes of identifying the bodies, is said to be the origin of "artificial memory"). Serres concludes that parasitism is "negentropic," the motor of change or invention—recalling Benjamin's art of interruption—consisting of a new logic with three elements: host, guest, and interrupter (noise is "the random element, transforming one system or one order into another"). The gram in the structure of language, and collage at the level of discourse, are operators of this inventive interruption.

This context provides an opportunity to demonstrate the usefulness of post-criticism not only as a compositional method but also as a method for reading paraliterature itself. I want to use the writings of John Cage as a test for allegorical reading, writings which in any case have exemplary value as some of the most important versions of paraliterature yet produced. Part of their value is that Cage is famous as a postmodernist musician. His "prepared piano" and early use of electronic equipment, along with his compositional innovations (graphic scores and aleatory procedures) and performance innovations (scores indeterminate as to performance), revolutionized—"postmodernized"—music. Students of post-criticism can benefit from the fact that Cage decided to apply his philosophy of composition to language ("I hope to let words exist, as I have tried to let sounds exist"[46]).

It is worth noting in this context that Cage, like Adorno, studied music theory with Schönberg. Cage adopted a view, similar to Adorno's strategy of the "concrete particular," that music should be a kind of research, an exploration of the logic of materials, which in Cage's case became extended to include not just the materials of music but everything in the natural and cultural worlds: "art changes because science changes—changes in science give artists different understandings of how nature works."[47] This attitude leads Cage to his own version—a musical one—of the "theoretical object":

> We know the air is filled with vibrations that we can't hear. In *Variations VII,* I tried to use sounds from that inaudible environment. But we can't consider that environment as an object. We know that it's a process. While in the case of the ashtray, we are indeed dealing with an object. It would be extremely interesting to place it in a little anechoic chamber and to listen to it through a suitable sound system. Object would become process; we would discover, thanks to a procedure borrowed from science, the meaning of nature through the music of objects (*Birds,* 221).

Moreover, this procedure is explicitly identified with the collage/montage principle, identified here as "silence" (or what Barthes calls the "death of the author"): "*The Gutenberg Galaxy* is made up of borrowings and collages: McLuhan applies what I call silence to all areas of knowledge, that is, he lets them speak. The death of the book is not the end of language: it continues. Just as in my case, silence has invaded everything, and there is still music" (*Birds,* 117). Cage acknowledges McLuhan, who has been credited with inventing a kind of "essai concret," and Norman O. Brown—both major representatives of post-critical writing—as important influences on his work.

Cage postmodernizes the critical essay by bringing to bear on its *inventio* and *dispositio* the same collage and aleatory procedures used in working with tape recorders and other electronic equipment in his musical compositions. The selection of the texts—Thoreau's Journals and Joyce's *Finnegans Wake*—is not itself random but, as in Derrida's selection of *Numbers,* a major part of the critical statement. (The Journals and the *Wake* are appropriated, literally or in a mimed version, and signed by Cage, remotivated as signifiers in a new frame.) Cage does not write about Thoreau, but uses the Journals for the generation of other texts which are in fact musicalized simulacra. These simulacra are collage constructions in that all the words, letters, phrases in them are derived directly from the Journals, selected according to chance operations. "Mureau" ("music" + "Thoreau"), for example, is "a mix of letters, syllables, words, phrases, and sentences. I wrote it by subjecting all the remarks of Henry David Thoreau about music, silence, and sounds he heard that are indexed in the Dover publications of the Journals to a series of *I Ching* chance operations. The personal pronoun was varied according to such operations and the typing was likewise determined." [48]

A more elaborate version of this operation, entitled *Empty Words,* reveals that such works are intended for performance, which is how Cage uses them to produce "lecture-events" (thus fulfilling the original logic of collage/montage which "represents" not in terms of *truth* but of *change*—indeed, the *I Ching* is the "book of changes"). "Subjecting Thoreau's writings to *I Ching* chance operations to obtain collage texts, I prepared parts for twelve speaker-vocalists (or -instrumentalists).... Along with these parts go recordings by Maryanne Amacher of breeze, rain and finally thunder and in the last (thunder) section a film by Luis Frangella representing lightning by means of briefly projected negatives of Thoreau's drawings." [49]

When confronting such a text in print, the full import of Barthes's advice about writerly reading becomes apparent, for something like "Mureau" may not be read "conceptually." Rather, by skimming the eye over the page, letting it be arrested momentarily by different typefaces so that the sense of those randomly noted words is allowed to register, a powerful effect emerges—the simulacrum of walking through the woods of Concord with the senses open and the attention floating. Cage explains that Thoreau listened "just as composers using technology nowadays listen; . . . and he explored the neighborhood of Concord with the same appetite with which they explore the possibilities provided by electronics."

Another example of Cage's procedure is *Writing for the Second Time through "Finnegans Wake."* This text was generated out of the *Wake* using Cage's mesostic form: "not acrostics: row down the middle, not down the edge. What makes a mesostic as far as I'm concerned is that the first letter of a word or name is on the first line and following it on the first line the second letter of the word or name is *not* to be found. (The second letter is on the second line)" (*Words,* 134). In this manner Cage produced, in his first version of the piece, one hundred fifteen pages of mesostics such as this one:

> Just
> A
> May i
> bE wrong!
> for She'll be sweet for you as i was sweet when
> i came down out of me mother.
> Jhem
> Or shen /brewed by arclight/
> and rorY end
> through all Christian
> ministrElsy.

By restricting further which syllables would be allowed, the second version was reduced to forty pages, of which Cage says:

> From time to time in the course of this work I've had my doubts about the validity of finding in *Finnegans Wake* these mesostics on his name which James Joyce didn't put there. However I just went straight on, A after J, E after M, J after S, Y after O, E after C. I read each passage at least three times and once or twice upside down (*Words,* 136).

If texts such as *Empty Words* exemplify the post-critical penchant for mimicry and collage, Cage's other writings display equally well the montage-allegory principle in a way that illuminates the allegorical power of the host-parasite theme. "Where Are We Eating? And What Are We Eating?" is a good example (an account of Cage's travels with Merce Cunningham's dance troupe entirely in terms of what they ordered when they stopped to eat) with which to mark the parallel between Cage's narrative allegory and Serres's *Parasite,* with the latter alerting us to the "extra" import of the many anecdotes concerned with guests, hosts, and dining to be found throughout Cage's writings. The extraordinary insight made available through Serres's elaboration of the French meaning of "parasite" (which means "noise" as well as "guest" and "parasite") is that Cage—who is famous as the composer who opened music to noise ("Since the theory of conventional music is a set of laws exclusively concerned with 'musical' sounds, having nothing to say about noises, it had been clear from the beginning that what was needed was a music based on noise, on noise's lawlessness.... The next steps were social"—*M,* v)—when he is writing about dining, is *still* talking about noise. His anecdotes about eating are the essayistic, discursive equivalents of utilizing noise in his musical compositions. They are also a commentary on the "parasitical" invention process of citation, upon which his music and essays depend.

At the center of this allegory about noise and dining is Cage's passion for mushrooms. Cage, founder of the New York Mycological Society, owned one of the world's largest private collections of books about mushrooms. Again, although anecdotes having to do with mushrooms are disseminated throughout Cage's writings, they are the exclusive topic in *Mushroom Book,* whose collage construction may be seen in this prospectus: "To finish for Lois programmed handwritten mushroom book including mushroom stories, excerpts from (mushroom) books, remarks about (mushroom) hunting, excerpts from Thoreau's *Journal* (fungi), excerpts from Thoreau's *Journal* (entire), remarks about: Life/Art, Art/Life, Life/Life, Art/Art, Zen, Current reading, Cooking (shopping, recipes), Games, Music mss., Maps, Friends, Invention, Projects, + Writing without syntax, Mesostics (on mushroom names)" (*M,* 133-34).

Why mushrooms? Cage remarks that it is because "mushroom" is next to "music" in most dictionaries. But read as paraliterature, the mushroom may be understood as a model mounted in a discourse for allegorical purposes. Indeed, the mushroom turns out to be the best emblem yet for what Derrida calls the "pharmakon," a potion or medicine which is at once elixir and poison (borrowed from Plato), modelling what Derrida calls (by analogy) "undecidables" (directed against all conceptual, classifying systems). The undecidables are:

> unities of simulacrum, "false" verbal properties (nominal or semantic) that can no longer be included within philosophical (binary) opposition, but which, however, inhabit philosophical opposition, resisting and disorganizing it, *without ever* constituting a third term, without ever leaving room for a solution in the form of speculative dialectics (the *pharmakon* is neither remedy nor poison, neither good nor evil, neither the inside nor the outside, neither speech nor writing (*Positions,* 43).

What the pharmakon is in the pharmaceutical (and the conceptual) realm, the mushroom is in the plant world, for, as Cage remarks, "the more you know them, the less sure you feel about identifying them. Each one is itself. Each mushroom is what it is—its own center. It's useless to pretend to know mushrooms. They escape your erudition" (*Birds*, 188). Cage's fascination with mycology is due in part to this undecidability of classification, as indicated in his anecdotes about experts who have misidentified poison species as edible, or of people who have become ill, even died, from eating a variety which had no effect on other people (different individuals react differently to the same species sometimes). When he suggests, in the context of anecdotes about his own experiences of poisoning by mushrooms, that it is too bad that books are not edible, Cage seems to be making a point similar to the one Barthes made in *S/Z* with respect to the *risk* in reading. Sarrasine, having mistaken the castrato Zambinella for a woman, dies "because of an inaccurate and inconclusive reasoning": "All the cultural codes, taken up from citation to citation, together form an oddly joined miniature version of encyclopedic knowledge, a farrago: this farrago forms the everyday 'reality' in relation to which the subject adapts himself, lives. One defect in this encyclopedia, one hole in this cultural fabric, and death can result. Ignorant of the code of Papal customs, Sarrasine dies from a gap in knowledge." [50] The mushroom, in other words, de-monstrates a lesson about survival.

According to the montage-allegory principle, Cage's mushroom anecdotes constitute collaged fragments alluding to the entire science of mycology. To determine the larger significance of the mushroom as allegory, then, one must review the "logic of the material" thus paradigmatically evoked (just as the absent terms of a semantic field are implied negatively by the specific term used in a sentence). The connotation relevant to our specific context has to do with the parasite-host relationship as a model for the status of the citation in post-criticism. The lesson taught by the kind of fungi hunted (emblematizing the research activity in general) and eaten by John Cage in particular—the fleshy, fruity, "higher" fungi, Boletus, Morels, and the like—is *symbiosis*. These fungi are not parasites, but *saprophytes* (any organism that lives on dead organic matter), and exist in a symbiotic, mutually beneficial relationship with their hosts (the green plants and trees which supply the organic "food"). The genus "Cortinarius," for example, as described by C.H. Kauffman (whose study, *The Agaricaceae of Michigan*, Cage lists among the ten books which most influenced him), may be found "in the region of pine and spruce, or in old beech forests, where the shade is dense and the ground is saturated with moisture," growing, of course, on a substratum of decaying matter. The trees benefit from the fungi growing among their roots by absorbing the nutrients made soluble as a result of the decomposing process to which the mushrooms contribute.[51]

This symbiotic ecology (related to the usefulness of the lower fungi, whose fermentations are essential to the production of wine, cheese and bread) is Cage's version of what Benjamin was talking about when he compared allegory to ruins, for it could be said that the saprophyte, living off the decay of dead organisms in a way that makes life possible for living plants, is to nature what the ruin is to culture, or the allegory to thought. For Adorno and Benjamin, the ruins were signs of the *decay* of the bourgeois era, requiring in philosophy a "logic of disintegration." For Derrida, too, deconstruction is a process of decomposition at work within the very *root* metaphores—the philosophemes—of Western thought. But we may see that this work is symbiotic, similar to the "mycorrhizal formation" in which tree roots and fungi supplement one another, enabling each to "live *on*," *sur*vive. The point is that if normal critics adhere to the model of the poem as living plant—the critic M.H. Abrams, for example, one of those accusing the deconstructors of being "parasites," whose *Mirror and the Lamp* provides the definitive study of the organic model in poetry—it might be useful to emblematize post-criticism as the saprophyte, growing among the roots of literature, feeding off the decay of tradition.

Cage suggests that his mushrooms could be read allegorically, even if he himself (being, as he says, the "grasshopper" of the fable) is too lazy to undertake the labor required for the comparison (*Silence,* 276). The social philosophy which he derives from his theory of music, however, manifests the symbiotic theme of ecology, of cooperation and an end to competition. For, as he warns, referring to the current world situation, to the same global implications of the parasite theme which inform Serres's study, "The party's nearly over. But the guests are going to stay: they have no place else to go. People who weren't invited are beginning to arrive. The house is a mess. We must all get together and without saying a word clean it up" (*M,* vii).

The immediate lesson for post-criticism, however, is found in this statement in the diary: "Mushrooms. Teaching-machines" (*M,* 196). In other words, what those who attack post-criticism as "parasitical" have not yet realized is that montage-allegory (the mushroom as teaching-machine) provides the very technique for popularization, for communicating the knowledge of the cultural disciplines to a general public, which the normal, so-called humanist critics claim to desire. Wayne Booth, in his recent Presidential address to the Modern Language Association, decried the drift of critical writing into solipsism, unaware that in *La Carte Postale,* to take just one example, Derrida makes available a working model capable of de-monstrating with utter simplicity the teleological essence of the logocentric tradition: "Everything in our bildopedic culture, in our encyclopedic politics, in our telecommunications of all kinds, in our telematicometaphysic archive, in our library, for example the marvelous Bodleian, everything is constructed on the protocolary charter of an axiom, which one could demonstrate, display on a card, a post card of course, it is so simple, elementary, brief, stereotyped" (*Carte,* 25)—that axiom being that Socrates comes *before* Plato, that the signified comes before the signifier; in short, the rigid order of an irreversible sequence. And when one mails a post card, confident that it will be delivered to the addressee, one displays the ideology of identity. Cage remarks that "Something needs to be done about the postal services. Either that or we should stop assuming just because we mailed something it will get where we sent it." [52] In *The Post Card* Derrida suggests the possibility of a communications network without "destiny" or "destination," in which all mail (messages) would be addressed only "to whom it may concern"—a system which values "noise" or invention over transparent meanings. Moreover, he shows us the writing which is appropriate for such an era: "It suffices to manipulate," he says, referring to the model post card, "to cut out, glue, and set going or parcel out, with hidden displacements and great tropic agility" (*Carte Postale,* 121). The image on the card (the one he found in the Bodleian library, depicting Socrates taking dictation from Plato) by means of *collage* becomes "articulate," "is capable of saying everything."

Such texts represent or mime not by means of signs but by signing—the signature. What remains of "identity" in a post-critical text is constituted by the new mimesis—the contamination between language and its user, the effects of which may be seen in the fact that the man who composed "Music of Changes," who composes all his productions by means of the "Book of Changes" (*I Ching*) in order, he hopes, to change society, is named *Jo Change* (John Cage).

References

1. Hayden White, *Tropics of Discourse* (Johns Hopkins: Baltimore, 1978), pp. 42-3, 45-7.
2. See Richard Kostelanetz, ed. *Esthetics Contemporary* (Prometheus: Buffalo, 1978).
3. Edward Fry, *Cubism* (McGraw-Hill: New York, n.d.), p. 27.
4. Eddie Wolfram, *History of Collage* (MacMillan: New York, 1975), pp. 17-18.
5. Group *Mu,* eds., *Collages* (Union Générale: Paris, 1978), pp. 13-14.
6. André Bazin, "The Ontology of the Photographic Image," in *Modern Culture and the Arts,* eds. James B. Hall, Barry Ulanov (McGraw-Hill: New York, 1972), p. 427.
7. *Collage et Montage au Théâtre et dans les autres Arts durant les Années Vingt* (La Cité: Lausanne, 1978), p. 98.
8. Benjamin, "The Author as Producer," in *The Essential Frankfurt School Reader,* eds A. Arato, E. Gebhardt (Urizen: New York, 1978), p. 266.
9. Roland Barthes, *Critique et Vérité* (Seuil: Paris, 1966), pp. 68-9. Also see Barthes, "The Structuralist Activity," in *The Structuralists: from Marx to Lévi-Strauss,* eds. R. and F. DeGeorge (Doubleday: Garden City, N.J., 1972), pp. 148-54.
10. The most recent statement of this generic conflation of literature and criticism is Rosalind Krauss's notion of "paraliterature." "If one of the tenets of modernist literature had been the creation of a work that would force reflection on the conditions of its own construction, that would insist on reading as a much more consciously *critical* act, then it is not surprising that the medium of a *post*modernist literature should be the critical text wrought

into a paraliterary form. And what is clear is that Barthes and Derrida are the *writers,* not the critics, that students now read." See Rosalind Krauss, "Poststructuralism and the 'Paraliterary,'" *October* 13 (1980): 40.

The insight of paraliterature is that although by the 1960s the collage revolution seemed to have run its course, it was in fact being renewed in critical discourse, which was itself finally being affected by experiments with representation. Indeed, as Elizabeth Bruss proposes in *Beautiful Theories* (concerned with the criticism of Susan Sontag, William Gass, Harold Bloom and Roland Barthes), theory is not only the most interesting of contemporary literary forms, it is the mode best suited for moving out of the impasse reached by the modernist movements in the arts.

11. See S. Doubrovsky, *Pourquoi la Nouvelle Critique?* (Mercure de France: Paris, 1966).

12. Derrida, "Living On: Borderlines," in *Deconstruction and Criticism* (Seabury: New York, 1979), pp. 94-5.

13. This is the topic of *Of Grammatology,* trans. Gayatari Spivak (Johns Hopkins: Baltimore, 1976).

14. Derrida, *Dissemination,* trans. Barbara Johnson (University of Chicago: Chicago, 1981), pp. 41-2.

15. Philip Lewis, "The Post-Structuralist Condition," *diacritics* 12 (1982): 16.

16. Derrida, *Positions,* trans. Alan Bass (University of Chicago: Chicago, 1981), p. 26.

17. Derrida, "Signature Event Context," in *Glyph* 1 (1977): 185.

18. Elsewhere Derrida writes: "What is in question here, this time at last, finds itself not displayed but given play, not staged but engaged, not demonstrated but *mounted,* mounted with a confectioner's skill in some implacable machinery" (*Dissemination,* 291). The verb is *monter,* from which "montage" derives. In a later text Derrida, playing on the meanings of *monter,* introduces the image of *passe-partout* or matting (used to frame pictures) as an analogy for the way a critical text "mounts" its examples. See Derrida, *La Vérité en Peinture* (Flammarion: Paris, 1978), pp. 5-18.

19. See Derrida, "Title (to be specified)," *Sub-Stance* 31 (1981).

20. This is the strategy used to deconstruct Kant in *La Vérité en Peinture* and Saussure in *Glas* (Galilée: Paris, 1974).

21. Derrida, "The Law of Genre," *Glyph* 7 (1980): 206.

22. "Dissemination" is written using the same montage technique practiced in *Numbers*—indeed, *Numbers* is selected as a tutor-text for just this reason—so that what is "remarked" here (the term Derrida prefers to "represented," "illustrated," "displayed," etc.) in the critical version is the structuration of the object of study: "We will hence be inscribing—simultaneously—in the angles and corners of these *Numbers,* within them and outside them, upon the stone that awaits *you,* certain questions that touch upon 'this' text 'here,' the status of its relation to *Numbers,* what it pretends to add to 'that' text in order to *mime* its presentations and representations, in order to seem to be offering some sort of review or account of it. For if *Numbers* offers an account of *itself* then 'this' text—and all that touches it—is already or still 'that' text. Just as *Numbers* calculates and feigns self-presentation and inscribes presence in a certain play, so too does what could still with a certain irony be called 'this' text mime the presentation, commentary, interpretation, review, account, or inventory of *Numbers.* As a *generalized simulacrum,* this writing circulates 'here' in the intertext of two fictions, between a so-called primary text and its so-called commentary" (*Dissemination,* 294).

23. Derrida, *Writing and Difference,* trans. Alan Bass (University of Chicago: Chicago, 1978), p. 296.

24. The very repetition that permits a sign to be a sign—to be recognized as the same as what it signifies—also produces a difference, as Saussure emphasized (the sign is not the referent itself). The temporal oscillation generated in this play between presence and absence is what Derrida terms *differance,* naming that which is opposed to the rigid first-second

ordering between signifier and signified dictated by logocentric semiotics from Plato to Saussure.

25. Derrida, *Speech and Phenomena,* trans. David Allison (Northwestern University: Evanston, 1973), p. 128.
26. Derrida, *La Carte Postale* (Flammarion: Paris, 1980), p. 317.
27. Wittgenstein, *Philosophical Investigations,* trans. G. Anscombe (Blackwell: Oxford, 1968), p. 105.
28. Craig Owens, "The Allegorical Impulse: Toward a Theory of Postmodernism," *October* 12 (1980): 84.
29. Owens, "The Allegorical Impulse (Part 2)," *October* 13 (1980): 79-80.
30. See Stephen Melville, "Notes on the Reemergence of Allegory," *October* 19 (1981); and Jonathan Culler, *On Deconstruction* (Cornell University: Ithaca, 1983).
31. Maureen Quilligan, *The Language of Allegory* (Cornell University: Ithaca, 1979), pp. 30-3.
32. Owens, "(Part 2)": 64, 66. Cf. Douglas Crimp, "The Photographic Activity of Postmodernism," *October* 15 (1980), for a discussion of Sherrie Levine, Benjamin.
33. Richard Kostelanetz, ed., *John Cage* (Praeger: New York, 1970), p. 115.
34. Barthes, *Roland Barthes,* trans. Richard Howard (Hill & Wang: New York, 1977), p. 90.
35. Stanley Mitchell, "Introduction," in Walter Benjamin, *Understanding Brecht,* trans. Anna Bostock (New Left Books: London, 1977), p. xiii.
36. Rainer Hoffmann, *Montage im Hohlraum zu Ernst Blochs "Spuren"* (Grundmann: Bonn, 1977), p. 92.
37. Benjamin, *"One-Way Street" and Other Writings,* trans. E. Jephcott, K. Shorter (New Left Books: London, 1979), p. 62.
38. Martin Jay, *The Dialectical Imagination* (Little Brown: Boston, 1973), pp. 176, 200. Jay mentions Norman O. Brown's *Love's Body* as perhaps a realization of Benjamin's plan.
39. Benjamin, *The Origin of German Tragic Drama,* trans. J. Osborne (New Left Books: London, 1977), p. 184.
40. Susan Buck-Morss, *The Origin of Negative Dialectics* (MacMillan: London, 1977), p. 56.
41. In Benjamin, "Short History of Photography," trans. Phil Patton, in *Artforum* 15 (1977): 50.
42. Derrida, *Spurs, Nietzsche's Styles,* trans. Barbara Harlow (University of Chicago: Chicago, 1979), p. 41.
43. In this case, Derrida appropriates the materials of a debate between Heidegger and Meyer Schapiro regarding the ownership of the shoes figured in Van Gogh's paintings—a theme which emblematizes the whole question of property and the signature involved in collage writing. Like the umbrella borrowed from Nietzsche, Van Gogh's shoes are detached from the critical argument and remotivated as a model for the gram—an act which by itself refutes the attempts of the critics to fix the shoe-signifier to a specific signified, to determine whether the pictured shoes were owned by a peasant woman (Heidegger) or by Van Gogh himself (Schapiro). Indeed the fact that the shoes are depicted as partially (un)laced is the clue to the process by which the gram-coupling works. "Like a lace, each 'thing,' each mode of being of the thing, passes inside then outside the other. We will often avail ourselves of this figure of the lace: passing and repassing through the eyelet of the thing, from outside in, from inside out, *over* the outer surface and *under* the inner one—and vice versa when this surface is turned inside out like the top of the left shoe, the lace remains the 'same' on both sides, shows itself and disappears (fort/da) in the regular crossing of the eyelet, insures the thing of its resemblance, bottoms tied to tops, inside fastened to outside, by a law of stricture." Derrida goes on to mock those who insist on viewing language in terms of the sign, seeing pairs (signifier-signified) everywhere, in the way that Heidegger and Schapiro assume they are looking at a pair of shoes. On close inspection of the paintings, Derrida argues wryly, it is not at all clear that the shoes are

matched; rather, they appear to be two left shoes—left behind, in any case, like Nietzsche's umbrella, for the next user, or writer. See Derrida, "Restitutions of Truth to Size," trans. John P. Leavey, Jr., in *Research in Phenomenology* 8 (1978): 32 (a partial translation of "Restitutions, de la vérité en pointure," in *Vérité en Peinture*).

44. J. Hillis Miller, "The Critic as Host," *Critical Inquiry* 3 (1977): 439.
45. Michel Serres, *The Parasite,* trans. Lawrence Schehr (Johns Hopkins: Baltimore, 1982) —Schehr's introduction, p. x.
46. John Cage (in conversation with Daniel Charles), *For the Birds* (Boyars: Boston, 1981), p. 151.
47. John Cage, *Silence* (M.I.T.: Cambridge, Massachusetts, 1961, 1970), p. 194.
48. Cage, *M: Writings '67-'72* (Wesleyan University: Middletown, 1974), p. i.
49. Cage, *Empty Words* (Wesleyan University: Middletown, 1981), p. 3.
50. Roland Barthes, *S/Z,* trans. Richard Miller (Hill & Wang: New York, 1974), pp. 184-85.
51. For a discussion of Mycology, see G.C. Ainsworth, *Introduction to the History of Mycology* (Cambridge University: Cambridge, 1976).
52. John Cage, *A Year From Monday* (Wesleyan University: Middletown, 1969), p. 150.

From
Hal Foster, ed.
The anti-aesthetic: essays
on postmodern culture
Port Townsend, WA.: Bay Press, 1983

Postmodernism and Consumer Society

FREDRIC JAMESON

The concept of postmodernism is not widely accepted or even understood today. Some of the resistance to it may come from the unfamiliarity of the works it covers, which can be found in all the arts: the poetry of John Ashbery, for instance, but also the much simpler talk poetry that came out of the reaction against complex, ironic, academic modernist poetry in the '60s; the reaction against modern architecture and in particular against the monumental buildings of the International Style, the pop buildings and decorated sheds celebrated by Robert Venturi in his manifesto, *Learning from Las Vegas*; Andy Warhol and Pop art, but also the more recent Photo-realism; in music, the moment of John Cage but also the later synthesis of classical and "popular" styles found in composers like Philip Glass and Terry Riley, and also punk and new-wave rock with such groups as the Clash, the Talking Heads and the Gang of Four; in film, everything that comes out of Godard—contemporary vanguard film and video—but also a whole new style of commercial or fiction films, which has its equivalent in contemporary novels as well, where the works of William Burroughs, Thomas Pynchon and Ishmael Reed on the one hand, and the French new novel on the other, are also to be numbered among the varieties of what can be called postmodernism.

This list would seem to make two things clear at once: first, most of the postmodernisms mentioned above emerge as specific reactions against the established forms of high modernism, against this or that dominant high modernism which conquered the university, the museum, the art gallery network, and the foundations. Those formerly subversive and embattled styles—Abstract Expressionism; the great modernist poetry of Pound, Eliot

This essay was originally a talk, portions of which were presented as a Whitney Museum Lecture in fall, 1982; it is published here essentially unrevised.

111

or Wallace Stevens; the International Style (Le Corbusier, Frank Lloyd Wright, Mies); Stravinsky; Joyce, Proust and Mann—felt to be scandalous or shocking by our grandparents are, for the generation which arrives at the gate in the 1960s, felt to be the establishment and the enemy—dead, stifling, canonical, the reified monuments one has to destroy to do anything new. This means that there will be as many different forms of postmodernism as there were high modernisms in place, since the former are at least initially specific and local reactions *against* those models. That obviously does not make the job of describing postmodernism as a coherent thing any easier, since the unity of this new impulse—if it has one—is given not in itself but in the very modernism it seeks to displace.

The second feature of this list of postmodernisms is the effacement in it of some key boundaries or separations, most notably the erosion of the older distinction between high culture and so-called mass or popular culture. This is perhaps the most distressing development of all from an academic standpoint, which has traditionally had a vested interest in preserving a realm of high or elite culture against the surrounding environment of philistinism, of schlock and kitsch, of TV series and *Reader's Digest* culture, and in transmitting difficult and complex skills of reading, listening and seeing to its initiates. But many of the newer postmodernisms have been fascinated precisely by that whole landscape of advertising and motels, of the Las Vegas strip, of the late show and Grade-B Hollywood film, of so-called paraliterature with its airport paperback categories of the gothic and the romance, the popular biography, the murder mystery and the science fiction or fantasy novel. They no longer "quote" such "texts" as a Joyce might have done, or a Mahler; they incorporate them, to the point where the line between high art and commercial forms seems increasingly difficult to draw.

A rather different indication of this effacement of the older categories of genre and discourse can be found in what is sometimes called contemporary theory. A generation ago there was still a technical discourse of professional philosophy—the great systems of Sartre or the phenomenologists, the work of Wittgenstein or analytical or common language philosophy—alongside which one could still distinguish that quite different discourse of the other academic disciplines—of political science, for example, or sociology or literary criticism. Today, increasingly, we have a kind of writing simply called "theory" which is all or none of those things at once. This new kind of discourse, generally associated with France and so-called French theory, is becoming widespread and marks the end of philosophy as such. Is the work of Michel Foucault, for example, to be called philosophy, history, social theory or political science? It's undecidable, as they say nowadays; and I will suggest that such "theoretical discourse" is also to be numbered among the manifestations of postmodernism.

Now I must say a word about the proper use of this concept: it is not just another word for the description of a particular style. It is also, at least in my use, a periodizing concept whose function is to correlate the emergence of new formal features in culture with the emergence of a new type of social life and a new economic order — what is often euphemistically called modernization, postindustrial or consumer society, the society of the media or the spectacle, or multinational capitalism. This new moment of capitalism can be dated from the postwar boom in the United States in the late 1940s and early '50s or, in France, from the establishment of the Fifth Republic in 1958. The 1960s are in many ways the key transitional period, a period in which the new international order (neocolonialism, the Green Revolution, computerization and electronic information) is at one and the same time set in place and is swept and shaken by its own internal contradictions and by external resistance. I want here to sketch a few of the ways in which the new postmodernism expresses the inner truth of that newly emergent social order of late capitalism, but will have to limit the description to only two of its significant features, which I will call pastiche and schizophrenia: they will give us a chance to sense the specificity of the postmodernist experience of space and time respectively.

One of the most significant features or practices in postmodernism today is pastiche. I must first explain this term, which people generally tend to confuse with or assimilate to that related verbal phenomenon called parody. Both pastiche and parody involve the imitation or, better still, the mimicry of other styles and particularly of the mannerisms and stylistic twitches of other styles. It is obvious that modern literature in general offers a very rich field for parody, since the great modern writers have all been defined by the invention or production of rather unique styles: think of the Faulknerian long sentence or of D. H. Lawrence's characteristic nature imagery; think of Wallace Stevens's peculiar way of using abstractions; think also of the mannerisms of the philosophers, of Heidegger for example, or Sartre; think of the musical styles of Mahler or Prokofiev. All of these styles, however different from each other, are comparable in this: each is quite unmistakable; once one is learned, it is not likely to be confused with something else.

Now parody capitalizes on the uniqueness of these styles and seizes on their idiosyncrasies and eccentricities to produce an imitation which mocks the original. I won't say that the satiric impulse is conscious in all forms of parody. In any case, a good or great parodist has to have some secret sympathy for the original, just as a great mimic has to have the capacity to put himself/herself in the place of the person imitated. Still, the general effect of parody is — whether in sympathy or with malice — to cast ridicule on the private nature of these stylistic mannerisms and their excessiveness and eccentricity with respect to the way people normally speak or write. So there remains somewhere behind all parody the feeling that there is a linguistic norm in contrast to which the styles of the great modernists can be mocked.

But what would happen if one no longer believed in the existence of normal language, of ordinary speech, of the linguistic norm (the kind of clarity and communicative power celebrated by Orwell in his famous essay, say)? One could think of it in this way: perhaps the immense fragmentation and privatization of modern literature — its explosion into a host of distinct private styles and mannerisms — foreshadows deeper and more general tendencies in social life as a whole. Supposing that modern art and modernism — far from being a kind of specialized aesthetic curiosity — actually anticipated social developments along these lines; supposing that in the decades since the emergence of the great modern styles society has itself begun to fragment in this way, each group coming to speak a curious private language of its own, each profession developing its private code or idiolect, and finally each individual coming to be a kind of linguistic island, separated from everyone else? But then in that case, the very possibility of any linguistic norm in terms of which one could ridicule private languages and idiosyncratic styles would vanish, and we would have nothing but stylistic diversity and heterogeneity.

That is the moment at which pastiche appears and parody has become impossible. Pastiche is, like parody, the imitation of a peculiar or unique style, the wearing of a stylistic mask, speech in a dead language: but it is a neutral practice of such mimicry, without parody's ulterior motive, without the satirical impulse, without laughter, without that still latent feeling that there exists something *normal* compared to which what is being imitated is rather comic. Pastiche is blank parody, parody that has lost its sense of humor: pastiche is to parody what that curious thing, the modern practice of a kind of blank irony, is to what Wayne Booth calls the stable and comic ironies of, say, the 18th century.

But now we need to introduce a new piece into this puzzle, which may help explain why classical modernism is a thing of the past and why postmodernism should have taken its place. This new component is what is generally called the "death of the subject" or, to say it in more conventional language, the end of individualism as such. The great modernisms were, as we have said, predicated on the invention of a personal, private style, as unmistakable as your fingerprint, as incomparable as your own body. But this means that the modernist aesthetic is in some way organically linked to the conception of a unique self and private identity, a unique personality and individuality, which can be expected to generate its own unique vision of the world and to forge its own unique, unmistakable style.

Yet today, from any number of distinct perspectives, the social theorists, the psychoanalysts, even the linguists, not to speak of those of us who work in the area of culture and cultural and formal change, are all exploring the notion that that kind of individualism and personal identity is a thing of the past; that the old individual or individualist subject is "dead"; and that one might even describe the concept of the unique individual and the theoretical basis of individualism as ideological. There are in fact two positions on all this, one of which is more radical than the other. The first one is content to say: yes, once upon a time, in the classic age of competitive capitalism, in the heyday of the nuclear family and the emergence of the bourgeoisie as the hegemonic social class, there was such a thing as individualism, as individual subjects. But today, in the age of corporate capitalism, of the so-called organization man, of bureaucracies in business as well as in the state, of demographic explosion—today, that older bourgeois individual subject no longer exists.

Then there is a second position, the more radical of the two, what one might call the poststructuralist position. It adds: not only is the bourgeois individual subject a thing of the past, it is also a myth; it *never* really existed in the first place; there have never been autonomous subjects of that type. Rather, this construct is merely a philosophical and cultural mystification which sought to persuade people that they "had" individual subjects and possessed this unique personal identity.

For our purposes, it is not particularly important to decide which of these positions is correct (or rather, which is more interesting and productive). What we have to retain from all this is rather an aesthetic dilemma: because if the experience and the ideology of the unique self, an experience and ideology which informed the stylistic practice of classical modernism, is over and done with, then it is no longer clear what the artists and writers of the present period are supposed to be doing. What is clear is merely that the older models—Picasso, Proust, T.S. Eliot—do not work any more (or are positively harmful), since nobody has that kind of unique private world and style to express any longer. And this is perhaps not merely a "psychological" matter: we also have to take into account the immense weight of seventy or eighty years of classical modernism itself. There is another sense in which the writers and artists of the present day will no longer be able to invent new styles and worlds—they've already been invented; only a limited number of combinations are possible; the most unique ones have been thought of already. So the weight of the whole modernist aesthetic tradition—now dead—also "weighs like a nightmare on the brains of the living," as Marx said in another context.

Hence, once again, pastiche: in a world in which stylistic innovation is no longer possible, all that is left is to imitate dead styles, to speak through the masks and with the voices of the styles in the imaginary museum. But this means that contemporary or postmodernist art is going to be about art itself in a new kind of way; even more, it means that one of its essential messages will involve the necessary failure of art and the aesthetic, the failure of the new, the imprisonment in the past.

As this may seem very abstract, I want to give a few examples, one of which is so omnipresent that we rarely link it with the kinds of developments in high art discussed here. This particular practice of pastiche is not high-cultural but very much within mass culture, and it is generally known as the "nostalgia film" (what the French neatly call *la mode rétro*—retrospective styling). We must conceive of this category in the broadest way: narrowly, no doubt, it consists merely of films about the past and about specific generational moments of that past. Thus, one of the inaugural films in this new "genre" (if that's what it is) was Lucas's *American Graffiti*, which in 1973 set out to recapture all the atmosphere and stylistic peculiarities of the 1950s United States, the United States of the Eisenhower era. Polanski's great film *Chinatown* does something similar for the 1930s, as does Bertolucci's *The Conformist* for the Italian and European context of the same period, the fascist era in Italy; and so forth. We could go on listing these films for some time: why call them pastiche? Are they not rather work in the more traditional genre known as the historical film—work which can more simply be theorized by extrapolating that other well-known form which is the historical novel?

I have my reasons for thinking that we need new categories for such films. But let me first add some anomalies: supposing I suggested that *Star Wars* is also a nostalgia film. What could that mean? I presume we can agree that this is not a historical film about our own intergalactic past. Let me put it somewhat differently: one of the most important cultural experiences of the generations that grew up from the '30s to the '50s was the Saturday after-noon serial of the Buck Rogers type—alien villians, true American heroes, heroines in distress, the death ray or the doomsday box, and the cliffhanger at the end whose miraculous resolution was to be witnessed next Saturday afternoon. *Star Wars* reinvents this experience in the form of a pastiche: that is, there is no longer any point to a parody of such serials since they are long extinct. *Star Wars*, far from being a pointless satire of such now dead forms, satisfies a deep (might I even say repressed?) longing to experience them again: it is a complex object in which on some first level children and adolescents can take the adventures straight, while the adult public is able to gratify a deeper and more properly nostalgic desire to return to that older period and to live its strange old aesthetic artifacts through once again. This film is thus *metonymically* a historical or nostalgia film: unlike *American Graffiti*, it does not reinvent a picture of the past in its lived totality; rather, by reinventing the feel and shape of characteristic art objects of an older period (the serials), it seeks to reawaken a sense of the past associated with those objects. *Raiders of the Lost Ark*, meanwhile, occupies an intermediary position here: on some level it is *about* the '30s and '40s, but in reality it too conveys that period metonymically through its own characteristic adventure stories (which are no longer ours).

Now let me discuss another interesting anomaly which may take us further towards understanding nostalgia film in particular and pastiche generally. This one involves a recent film called *Body Heat,* which, as has abundantly been pointed out by the critics, is a kind of distant remake of *The Postman Always Rings Twice* or *Double Indemnity.* (The allusive and elusive plagiarism of older plots is, of course, also a feature of pastiche.) Now *Body Heat* is technically not a nostalgia film, since it takes place in a contemporary setting, in a little Florida village near Miami. On the other hand, this technical contemporaneity is most ambiguous indeed: the credits —always our first cue—are lettered and scripted in a '30s Art-Deco style which cannot but trigger nostalgic reactions (first to *Chinatown,* no doubt, and then beyond it to some more historical referent). Then the very style of the hero himself is ambiguous: William Hurt is a new star but has nothing of the distinctive style of the preceding generation of male superstars like Steve McQueen or even Jack Nicholson, or rather, his persona here is a kind of mix of their characteristics with an older role of the type generally associated with Clark Gable. So here too there is a faintly archaic feel to all this. The spectator begins to wonder why this story, which could have been situated anywhere, is set in a small Florida town, in spite of its contemporary reference. One begins to realize after a while that the small town setting has a crucial strategic function: it allows the film to do without most of the signals and references which we might associate with the contemporary world, with consumer society—the appliances and artifacts, the high rises, the object world of late capitalism. Technically, then, its objects (its cars, for instance) are 1980s products, but everything in the film conspires to blur that immediate contemporary reference and to make it possible to receive this too as nostalgia work—as a narrative set in some indefinable nostalgic past, an eternal '30s, say, beyond history. It seems to me exceedingly symptomatic to find the very style of nostalgia films invading and colonizing even those movies today which have contemporary settings: as though, for some reason, we were unable today to focus our own present, as though we have become incapable of achieving aesthetic representations of our own current experience. But if that is so, then it is a terrible indictment of consumer capitalism itself—or at the very least, an alarming and pathological symptom of a society that has become incapable of dealing with time and history.

So now we come back to the question of why nostalgia film or pastiche is to be considered different from the older historical novel or film (I should also include in this discussion the major literary example of all this, to my mind the novels of E.L. Doctorow—*Ragtime,* with its turn-of-the-century atmosphere, and *Loon Lake,* for the most part about our 1930s. But these are, to my mind, historical novels in appearance only. Doctorow is a serious artist and one of the few genuinely Left or radical novelists at work today. It is no disservice to him, however, to suggest that his narratives do not represent our historical past so much as they represent our ideas or cultural stereotypes about that past.) Cultural production has been driven back inside the mind, within the monadic subject: it can no longer look directly out of its eyes at the real world for the referent but must, as in Plato's cave, trace its mental images of the world on its confining walls. If there is any realism left here, it is a "realism" which springs from the shock of grasping that confinement and of realizing that, for whatever peculiar reasons, we seem condemned to seek the historical past through our own pop images and stereotypes about that past, which itself remains forever out of reach.

I now want to turn to what I see as the second basic feature of postmodernism, namely its peculiar way with time—which one could call "textuality" or "écriture" but which I have found it useful to discuss in terms of current theories of schizophrenia. I hasten to forestall any number of possible misconceptions about my use of this word: it is meant to be descriptive and not diagnostic. I am very far indeed from believing that any of the most significant postmodernist artists—John Cage, John Ashbery, Philippe Sollers, Robert Wilson, Andy Warhol, Ishmael Reed, Michael Snow, even Samuel Beckett himself—are in any sense schizophrenics. Nor is the point some culture-and-personality diagnosis of our society and its art: there are, one would think, far more damaging things to be said about our social system than are available by the use of pop psychology. I'm not even sure that the view of schizophrenia I'm about to outline—a view largely developed in the work of the French psychoanalyst Jacques Lacan—is clinically accurate; but that doesn't matter either, for my purposes.

The originality of Lacan's thought in this area is to have considered schizophrenia essentially as a language disorder and to have linked schizophrenic experience to a whole view of language acquisition as the fundamental missing link in the Freudian conception of the formation of the mature psyche. He does this by giving us a linguistic version of the Oedipus complex in which the Oedipal rivalry is described in terms not of the biological individual who is the rival for the mother's attention, but rather of what he calls the Name-of-the-Father, paternal authority now considered as linguistic function. What we need to retain from this is the idea that psychosis, and more particularly schizophrenia, emerges from the failure of the infant to accede fully into the realm of speech and language.

As for language, Lacan's model is the now orthodox structuralist one, which is based on a conception of a linguistic sign as having two (or perhaps three) components. A sign, a word, a text, is here modelled as a relationship between a signifier—a material object, the sound of a word, the script of a text—and a signified, the *meaning* of that material word or material text. The third component would be the so-called "referent," the "real" object in the "real" world to which the sign refers—the real cat as opposed to the concept of a cat or the sound "cat." But for structuralism in general there has been a tendency to feel that reference is a kind of myth, that one can no longer talk about the "real" in that external or objective way. So we are left with the sign itself and its two components. Meanwhile, the other thrust of structuralism has been to try to dispel the old conception of language as naming (e.g., God gave Adam language in order to name the beasts and plants in the Garden), which involves a one-to-one correspondence between a signifier and a signified. Taking a structural view, one comes quite rightly to feel that sentences don't work that way: we don't translate the individual signifiers or words that make up a sentence back into their signifieds on a one-to-one basis. Rather, we read the whole sentence, and it is from the interrelationship of its words or signifiers that a more global meaning—now called a "meaning-effect"—is derived. The signified—maybe even the illusion or the mirage of the signified and of meaning in general—is an effect produced by the interrelationship of material signifiers.

All of this puts us in the position of grasping schizophrenia as the breakdown of the relationship between signifiers. For Lacan, the experience of temporality, human time, past, present, memory, the persistence of personal identity over months and years—this existential or experiential feeling of time itself—is also an effect of language. It is because language has a past and a future, because the sentence moves in time, that we can have what seems to us a concrete or lived experience of time. But since the schizophrenic does not know language articulation in that way, he or she does not have our experience of temporal continuity either, but is condemned to live a perpetual present with which the various moments of his or her past have little connection and for which there is no conceivable future on the horizon. In other words, schizophrenic experience is an experience of isolated, disconnected, discontinuous material signifiers which fail to link up into a coherent sequence. The schizophrenic thus does not know personal identity in our sense, since our feeling of identity depends on our sense of the persistence of the "I" and the "me" over time.

On the other hand, the schizophrenic will clearly have a far more intense experience of any given present of the world than we do, since our own present is always part of some larger set of projects which force us selectively to focus our perceptions. We do not, in other words, simply globally receive the outside world as an undifferentiated vision: we are always engaged in using it, in threading certain paths through it, in attending to this or that object or person within it. The schizophrenic, however, is not only "no one" in the sense of having no personal identity; he or she also does nothing, since to have a project means to be able to commit oneself to a certain continuity over time. The schizophrenic is thus given over to an undifferentiated vision of the world in the present, a by no means pleasant experience:

> I remember very well the day it happened. We were staying in the country and I had gone for a walk alone as I did now and then. Suddenly, as I was passing the school, I heard a German song; the children were having a singing lesson. I stopped to listen, and at that instant a strange feeling came over me, a feeling hard to analyze but akin to something I was to know too well later—a disturbing sense of unreality. It seemed to me that I no longer recognized the school, it had become as large as a barracks; the singing children were prisoners, compelled to sing. It was as though the school and the children's song were apart from the rest of the world. At the same time my eye encountered a field of wheat whose limits I could not see. The yellow vastness, dazzling in the sun, bound up with the song of the children imprisoned in the smooth stone school-barracks, filled me with such anxiety that I broke into sobs. I ran home to our garden and began to play "to make things seem as they usually were," that is, to return to reality. It was the first appearance of those elements which were always present in later sensations of unreality: illimitable vastness, brilliant light, and the gloss and smoothness of material things. (Renee Sechehaye, *Autobiography of a Schizophrenic Girl.*)

Note that as temporal continuities break down, the experience of the present becomes powerfully, overwhelmingly vivid and "material": the world comes before the schizophrenic with heightened intensity, bearing a mysterious and oppressive charge of affect, glowing with hallucinatory energy. But what might for us seem a desirable experience—an increase in our perceptions, a libidinal or hallucinogenic intensification of our normally humdrum and familiar surroundings—is here felt as loss, as "unreality."

What I want to underscore, however, is precisely the way in which the signifier in isolation becomes ever more material—or, better still, *literal*— ever more vivid in sensory ways, whether the new experience is attractive or terrifying. We can show the same thing in the realm of language: what the schizophrenic breakdown of language does to the individual words that remain behind is to reorient the subject or the speaker to a more literalizing attention towards those words. Again, in normal speech, we try to see through the materiality of words (their strange sounds and printed appearance, my voice timbre and peculiar accent, and so forth) towards their meaning. As meaning is lost, the materiality of words becomes obsessive, as is the case when children repeat a word over and over again until its sense is lost and it becomes an incomprehensible incantation. To begin to link up with our earlier description, a signifier that has lost its signified has thereby been transformed into an image.

This long digression on schizophrenia has allowed us to add a feature that we could not quite handle in our earlier description—namely time itself. We must therefore now shift our discussion of postmodernism from the visual arts to the temporal ones—to music, poetry and certain kinds of narrative texts like those of Beckett. Anyone who has listened to John Cage's music may well have had an experience similar to those just evoked: frustration and desperation—the hearing of a single chord or note followed by a silence so long that memory cannot hold on to what went before, a silence then banished into oblivion by a new strange sonorous present which itself disappears. This experience could be illustrated by many forms of cultural production today. I have chosen a text by a younger poet, partly because his "group" or "school"—known as the Language Poets—has in many ways made the experience of temporal discontinuity—the experience described here in terms of schizophrenic language—central to their language experiments and to what they like to call the "New Sentence." This is a poem called "China" by Bob Perelman (it can be found in his recent collection *Primer,* published by This Press in Berkeley, California):

We live on the third world from the sun. Number three. Nobody tells us what to do.

The people who taught us to count were being very kind.

It's always time to leave.

If it rains, you either have your umbrella or you don't.

The wind blows your hat off.

The sun rises also.

I'd rather the stars didn't describe us to each other; I'd rather we do it for ourselves.

Run in front of your shadow.

A sister who points to the sky at least once a decade is a good sister.

The landscape is motorized.

The train takes you where it goes.

Bridges among water.

Folks straggling along vast stretches of concrete, heading into the plane.

Don't forget what your hat and shoes will look like when you are nowhere to be found.

Even the words floating in air make blue shadows.

If it tastes good we eat it.

The leaves are falling. Point things out.

Pick up the right things.

Hey guess what? What? *I've learned how to talk.* Great.

The person whose head was incomplete burst into tears.

As it fell, what could the doll do? Nothing.

Go to sleep.

You look great in shorts. And the flag looks great too.

Everyone enjoyed the explosions.

Time to wake up.

But better get used to dreams.

Now one may object that this is not exactly schizophrenic writing in the clinical sense; it does not seem quite right to say that these sentences are free-floating material signifiers whose signifieds have evaporated. There does seem to be some global meaning here. Indeed, insofar as this is in some curious and secret way a political poem, it does seem to capture some of the excitement of the immense and unfinished social experiment of the new China, unparalleled in world history: the unexpected emergence, between the two superpowers, of "number three;" the freshness of a whole new object-world produced by human beings in some new control over their own collective destiny; the signal event, above all, of a collectivity which has become a new "subject of history" and which, after the long subjection of feudalism and imperialism, speaks in its own voice, for itself, for the first time ("Hey guess what?...I've learned how to talk."). Yet such meaning floats over the text or behind it. One cannot, I think, read this text according to any of the older New-Critical categories and find the complex inner relationships and texture which characterized the older "concrete universal" of classical modernisms such as Wallace Stevens's.

Perelman's work, and Language Poetry generally, owes something to Gertrude Stein and, beyond her, to certain aspects of Flaubert. So it is not inappropriate at this point to insert an old account of Flaubert's sentences by Sartre, which conveys a vivid feeling of the movement of such sentences:

> His sentence closes in on the object, seizes it, immobilizes it, and breaks its back, wraps itself around it, changes into stone and petrifies its object along with itself. It is blind and deaf, bloodless, not a breath of life; a deep silence separates it from the sentence which follows; it falls into the void, eternally, and drags its prey down into that infinite fall. Any reality, once described, is struck off the inventory. (Jean-Paul Sartre, *What Is Literature?*)

The description is a hostile one, and the liveliness of Perelman is historically rather different from this homicidal Flaubertian practice. (For Mallarmé, Barthes once observed in a similar vein, the sentence, the word, is a way of murdering the outside world.) Yet it conveys some of the mystery of sentences that fall into a void of silence so great that for a time one wonders whether any new sentence could possibly emerge to take their place.

But now the secret of this poem must be disclosed. It is a little like Photo-realism, which looked like a return to representation after the anti-representational abstractions of Abstract Expressionism, until people began to realize that these paintings are not exactly realistic either, since what they represent is not the outside world but rather only a photograph of the outside world or, in other words, the latter's image. False realisms, they are really art about other art, images of other images. In the present case, the represented object is not really China after all: what happened was that Perelman came across a book of photographs in a stationery store in Chinatown, a book whose captions and characters obviously remained dead letters (or should one say material signifiers?) to him. The sentences of the poem are *his* captions to those pictures. Their referents are other images, another text, and the "unity" of the poem is not *in* the text at all but outside it in the bound unity of an absent book.

Now I must try very rapidly in conclusion to characterize the relationship of cultural production of this kind to social life in this country today. This will also be the moment to address the principal objection to concepts of post-modernism of the type I have sketched here: namely that all the features we have enumerated are not new at all but abundantly characterized modernism proper or what I call high-modernism. Was not Thomas Mann, after all, interested in the idea of pastiche, and are not certain chapters of *Ulysses* its most obvious realization? Did we not mention Flaubert, Mallarmé and Gertrude Stein in our account of postmodernist temporality? What is so new about all of this? Do we really need the concept of a *post*modernism?

One kind of answer to this question would raise the whole issue of peri-odization and of how a historian (literary or other) posits a radical break between two henceforth distinct periods. I must limit myself to the sugges-tion that radical breaks between periods do not generally involve complete changes of content but rather the restructuration of a certain number of elements already given: features that in an earlier period or system were subordinate now become dominant, and features that had been dominant again become secondary. In this sense, everything we have described here can be found in earlier periods and most notably within modernism proper: my point is that until the present day those things have been secondary or minor features of modernist art, marginal rather than central, and that we have something new when they become the central features of cultural production.

But I can argue this more concretely by turning to the relationship be-tween cultural production and social life generally. The older or classical modernism was an oppositional art; it emerged within the business society of

the gilded age as scandalous and offensive to the middle-class public—
ugly, dissonant, bohemian, sexually shocking. It was something to make
fun of (when the police were not called in to seize the books or close the
exhibitions): an offense to good taste and to common sense, or, as Freud and
Marcuse would have put it, a provocative challenge to the reigning reality-
and performance-principles of early 20th-century middle-class society.
Modernism in general did not go well with overstuffed Victorian furniture,
with Victorian moral taboos, or with the conventions of polite society. This
is to say that whatever the explicit political content of the great high
modernisms, the latter were always in some mostly implicit ways dangerous
and explosive, subversive within the established order.

If then we suddenly return to the present day, we can measure the immen-
sity of the cultural changes that have taken place. Not only are Joyce and
Picasso no longer weird and repulsive, they have become classics and now
look rather realistic to us. Meanwhile, there is very little in either the form or
the content of contemporary art that contemporary society finds intolerable
and scandalous. The most offensive forms of this art—punk rock, say, or
what is called sexually explicit material—are all taken in stride by society,
and they are commercially successful, unlike the productions of the older
high modernism. But this means that even if contemporary art has all the
same formal features as the older modernism, it has still shifted its position
fundamentally within our culture. For one thing, commodity production and
in particular our clothing, furniture, buildings and other artifacts are now
intimately tied in with styling changes which derive from artistic experi-
mentation; our advertising, for example, is fed by postmodernism in all the
arts and inconceivable without it. For another, the classics of high modernism are now part of the so-called canon and are taught in schools and universities—which at once empties them of any of their older subversive
power. Indeed, one way of marking the break between the periods and of
dating the emergence of postmodernism is precisely to be found there: in the
moment (the early 1960s, one would think) in which the position of high
modernism and its dominant aesthetics become established in the academy
and are henceforth felt to be academic by a whole new generation of poets,
painters and musicians.

But one can also come at the break from the other side, and describe it in
terms of periods of recent social life. As I have suggested, non-Marxists and
Marxists alike have come around to the general feeling that at some point
following World War II a new kind of society began to emerge (variously
described as postindustrial society, multinational capitalism, consumer
society, media society and so forth). New types of consumption; planned
obsolescence; an ever more rapid rhythm of fashion and styling changes; the
penetration of advertising, television and the media generally to a hitherto
unparalleled degree throughout society; the replacement of the old tension

between city and country, center and province, by the suburb and by universal standardization; the growth of the great networks of superhighways and the arrival of automobile culture—these are some of the features which would seem to mark a radical break with that older prewar society in which high modernism was still an underground force.

I believe that the emergence of postmodernism is closely related to the emergence of this new moment of late, consumer or multinational capitalism. I believe also that its formal features in many ways express the deeper logic of that particular social system. I will only be able, however, to show this for one major theme: namely the disappearance of a sense of history, the way in which our entire contemporary social system has little by little begun to lose its capacity to retain its own past, has begun to live in a perpetual present and in a perpetual change that obliterates traditions of the kind which all earlier social formations have had in one way or another to preserve. Think only of the media exhaustion of news: of how Nixon and, even more so, Kennedy are figures from a now distant past. One is tempted to say that the very function of the news media is to relegate such recent historical experiences as rapidly as possible into the past. The informational function of the media would thus be to help us forget, to serve as the very agents and mechanisms for our historical amnesia.

But in that case the two features of postmodernism on which I have dwelt here—the transformation of reality into images, the fragmentation of time into a series of perpetual presents—are both extraordinarily consonant with this process. My own conclusion here must take the form of a question about the critical value of the newer art. There is some agreement that the older modernism functioned against its society in ways which are variously described as critical, negative, contestatory, subversive, oppositional and the like. Can anything of the sort be affirmed about postmodernism and its social moment? We have seen that there is a way in which postmodernism replicates or reproduces—reinforces—the logic of consumer capitalism; the more significant question is whether there is also a way in which it resists that logic. But that is a question we must leave open.

The Ecstasy of Communication

JEAN BAUDRILLARD

There is no longer any system of objects. My first book contains a critique of the object as obvious fact, subtance, reality, use value.[1] There the object was taken as sign, but as sign still heavy with meaning. In this critique two principal logics interfered with each other: a phantasmatic logic *that referred principally to psychoanalysis — its identifications, projections, and the entire imaginary realm of transcendence, power and sexuality operating at the level of objects and the environment, with a privilege accorded to the house/automobile axis (immanence/transcendence); and a* differential social logic *that made distinctions by referring to a sociology, itself derived from anthropology (consumption as the production of signs, differentiation, status and prestige). Behind these logics, in some way descriptive and analytic, there was already the dream of symbolic exchange, a dream of the status of the object and consumption beyond exchange and use, beyond value and equivalence. In other words,* a sacrificial logic *of consumption, gift, expenditure* (dépense), *potlatch, and the accursed portion.[2]*

In a certain way all this still exists, and yet in other respects it is all disappearing. The description of this whole intimate universe — projective, imaginary and symbolic — still corresponded to the object's status as mirror of the subject, and that in turn to the imaginary depths of the mirror and "scene": there is a domestic scene, a scene of interiority, a private space-time (correlative, moreover, to a public space). The oppositions subject/object and public/private were still meaningful. This was the era of the discovery and exploration of daily life, this other scene emerging in the shadow of the historic scene, with the former receiving more and more symbolic investment as the latter was politically disinvested.

But today the scene and mirror no longer exist; instead, there is a screen and network. In place of the reflexive transcendence of mirror and scene,

126

there is a nonreflecting surface, an immanent surface where operations unfold—the smooth operational surface of communication.

Something has changed, and the Faustian, Promethean (perhaps Oedipal) period of production and consumption gives way to the "proteinic" era of networks, to the narcissistic and protean era of connections, contact, contiguity, feedback and generalized interface that goes with the universe of communication. With the television image—the television being the ultimate and perfect object for this new era—our own body and the whole surrounding universe become a control screen.

If one thinks about it, people no longer project themselves into their objects, with their affects and their representations, their fantasies of possession, loss, mourning, jealousy: the psychological dimension has in a sense vanished, and even if it can always be marked out in detail, one feels that it is not really there that things are being played out. Roland Barthes already indicated this some time ago in regard to the automobile: little by little a logic of "driving" has replaced a very subjective logic of possession and projection.[3] No more fantasies of power, speed and appropriation linked to the object itself, but instead a tactic of potentialities linked to usage: mastery, control and command, an optimalization of the play of possibilities offered by the car as vector and vehicle, and no longer as object of psychological sanctuary. The subject himself, suddenly transformed, becomes a computer at the wheel, not a drunken demiurge of power. The vehicle now becomes a kind of capsule, its dashboard the brain, the surrounding landscape unfolding like a televised screen (instead of a live-in projectile as it was before).

(But we can conceive of a stage beyond this one, where the car is still a vehicle of performance, a stage where it becomes an information network. The famous Japanese car that talks to you, that "spontaneously" informs you of its general state and even of your general state, possibly refusing to function if you are not functioning well, the car as deliberating consultant and partner in the general negotiation of a lifestyle, something—or someone: at this point there is no longer any difference—with which you are connected. The fundamental issue becomes the communication with the car itself, a perpetual test of the subject's presence with his own objects, an uninterrupted interface.

It is easy to see that from this point speed and displacement no longer matter. Neither does unconscious projection, nor an individual or social type of competition, nor prestige. Besides, the car began to be de-sacralized in this sense some time ago: it's all over with speed—I drive more and consume less. Now, however, it is an ecological ideal that installs itself at every level. No more expenditure, consumption, performance, but instead regulation, well-tempered functionality, solidarity among all the elements of the same system, control and global management of an ensemble. Each system, including no doubt the domestic universe, forms a sort of ecological niche where the essential thing is to maintain a relational decor, where all the terms must continually communicate among themselves and stay in contact, informed of the respective condition of the others and of the system as a whole, where opacity, resistance or the secrecy of a single term can lead to catastrophe.) [4]

Private "telematics": each person sees himself at the controls of a hypothetical machine, isolated in a position of perfect and remote sovereignty, at an infinite distance from his universe of origin. Which is to say, in the exact position of an astronaut in his capsule, in a state of weightlessness that necessitates a perpetual orbital flight and a speed sufficient to keep him from crashing back to his planet of origin.

This realization of a living satellite, *in vivo* in a quotidian space, corresponds to the satellitization of the real, or what I call the "hyperrealism of simulation" [5]: the elevation of the domestic universe to a spatial power, to a spatial metaphor, with the satellitization of the two-room-kitchen-and-bath put into orbit in the last lunar module. The very quotidian nature of the terrestrial habitat hypostasized in space means the end of metaphysics. The era of hyperreality now begins. What I mean is this: what was projected psychologically and mentally, what used to be lived out on earth as metaphor, as mental or metaphorical scene, is henceforth projected into reality, without any metaphor at all, into an absolute space which is also that of simulation.

This is only an example, but it signifies as a whole the passage into orbit, as orbital and environmental model, of our private sphere itself. It is no longer a scene where the dramatic interiority of the subject, engaged with its objects as with its image, is played out. We are here at the controls of a micro-satellite, in orbit, living no longer as an actor or dramaturge but as a terminal of multiple networks. Television is still the most direct prefiguration of this. But today it is the very space of habitation that is conceived as both receiver and distributor, as the space of both reception and operations, the control screen and terminal which as such may be endowed with telematic power—that is, with the capability of regulating everything from a distance, including work in the home and, of course, consumption, play, social relations and leisure. Simulators of leisure or of vacations in the home—like flight simulators for airplane pilots—become conceivable.

Here we are far from the living-room and close to science fiction. But once more it must be seen that all these changes—the decisive mutations of objects and of the environment in the modern era—have come from an irreversible tendency towards three things: an ever greater formal and operational abstraction of elements and functions and their homogenization in a single virtual process of functionalization; the displacement of bodily movements and efforts into electric or electronic commands, and the miniaturization, in time and space, of processes whose real scene (though it is no longer a scene) is that of infinitesimal memory and the screen with which they are equipped.

There is a problem here, however, to the extent that this electronic "encephalization" and miniaturization of circuits and energy, this transistorization of the environment, relegates to total uselessness, desuetude and almost obscenity all that used to fill the scene of our lives. It is well known how the simple presence of the television changes the rest of the habitat into a kind of archaic envelope, a vestige of human relations whose very survival remains perplexing. As soon as this scene is no longer haunted by its actors and their fantasies, as soon as behavior is crystallized on certain screens and operational terminals, what's left appears only as a large useless body, deserted and condemned. The real itself appears as a large useless body.

This is the time of miniaturization, telecommand and the microprocession of time, bodies, pleasures. There is no longer any ideal principle for these things at a higher level, on a human scale. What remains are only concentrated effects, miniaturized and immediately available. This change from human scale to a system of nuclear matrices is visible everywhere: this body, our body, often appears simply superfluous, basically useless in its extension, in the multiplicity and complexity of its organs, its tissues and functions, since today everything is concentrated in the brain and in genetic codes, which alone sum up the operational definition of being. The countryside, the immense geographic countryside, seems to be a deserted body whose expanse and dimensions appear arbitrary (and which is boring to cross even if one leaves the main highways), as soon as all events are epitomized in the towns, themselves undergoing reduction to a few miniaturized highlights. And time: what can be said about this immense free time we are left with, a dimension henceforth useless in its unfolding, as soon as the instantaneity of communication has miniaturized our exchanges into a succession of instants?

Thus the body, landscape, time all progressively disappear as scenes. And the same for public space: the theater of the social and theater of politics are both reduced more and more to a large soft body with many heads. Advertising in its new version—which is no longer a more or less baroque, utopian or ecstatic scenario of objects and consumption, but the effect of an omnipresent visibility of enterprises, brands, social interlocuters and the social virtues of communication—advertising in its new dimension invades everything, as public space (the street, monument, market, scene) disappears. It realizes, or, if one prefers, it materializes in all its obscenity; it monopolizes public life in its exhibition. No longer limited to its traditional language, advertising organizes the architecture and realization of super-objects like Beaubourg and the Forum des Halles, and of future projects (e.g., Parc de la Villette) which are monuments (or anti-monuments) to advertising, not because they will be geared to consumption but because they are immediately proposed as an anticipated demonstration of the operation of culture, commodities, mass movement and social flux. It is our only architecture today: great screens on which are reflected atoms, particles, molecules in motion. Not a public scene or true public space but gigantic spaces of circulation, ventilation and ephemeral connections.

It is the same for private space. In a subtle way, this loss of public space occurs contemporaneously with the loss of private space. The one is no longer a spectacle, the other no longer a secret. Their distinctive opposition, the clear difference of an exterior and an interior exactly described the domestic *scene* of objects, with its rules of play and limits, and the sovereignty of a symbolic space which was also that of the subject. Now this opposition is effaced in a sort of *obscenity* where the most intimate processes of our life become the virtual feeding ground of the media (the Loud family in the United States, the innumerable slices of peasant or patriarchal life on French television). Inversely, the entire universe comes to unfold arbitrarily on your domestic screen (all the useless information that comes to you from the entire world, like a microscopic pornography of the universe, useless, excessive, just like the sexual close-up in a porno film): all this explodes the scene formerly preserved by the minimal separation of public and private, the scene that was played out in a restricted space, according to a secret ritual known only by the actors.

Certainly, this private universe was alienating to the extent that it separated you from others—or from the world, where it was invested as a protective enclosure, an imaginary protector, a defense system. But it also reaped the symbolic benefits of alienation, which is that the Other exists, and that otherness can fool you for the better or the worse. Thus consumer society lived also under the sign of alienation, as a society of the spectacle.[6] But just so: as long as there is alienation, there is spectacle, action, scene. It is not obscenity—the spectacle is never obscene. Obscenity begins precisely when there is no more spectacle, no more scene, when all becomes transparence and immediate visibility, when everything is exposed to the harsh and inexorable light of information and communication.

We are no longer a part of the drama of alienation; we live in the ecstasy of communication. And this ecstasy is obscene. The obscene is what does away with every mirror, every look, every image. The obscene puts an end to every representation. But it is not only the sexual that becomes obscene in pornography; today there is a whole pornography of information and communication, that is to say, of circuits and networks, a pornography of all functions and objects in their readability, their fluidity, their availability, their regulation, in their forced signification, in their performativity, in their branching, in their polyvalence, in their free expression....

It is no longer then the traditional obscenity of what is hidden, repressed, forbidden or obscure; on the contrary, it is the obscenity of the visible, of the all-too-visible, of the more-visible-than-the-visible. It is the obscenity of what no longer has any secret, of what dissolves completely in information and communication.

Marx set forth and denounced the obscenity of the commodity, and this obscenity was linked to its equivalence, to the abject principle of free circulation, beyond all use value of the object. The obscenity of the commodity stems from the fact that it is abstract, formal and light in opposition to the weight, opacity and substance of the object. The commodity is readable: in opposition to the object, which never completely gives up its secret, the commodity always manifests its visible essence, which is its price. It is the formal place of transcription of all possible objects; through it, objects communicate. Hence, the commodity form is the first great medium of the modern world. But the message that the objects deliver through it is already extremely simplified, and it is always the same: their exchange value. Thus at bottom the message already no longer exists; it is the medium that imposes itself in its pure circulation. This is what I call (potentially) ecstasy.

One has only to prolong this Marxist analysis, or push it to the second or third power, to grasp the transparence and obscenity of the universe of communication, which leaves far behind it those relative analyses of the universe of the commodity. All functions abolished in a single dimension, that of communication. That's the ecstasy of communication. All secrets, spaces and scenes abolished in a single dimension of information. That's obscenity.

The hot, sexual obscenity of former times is succeeded by the cold and communicational, contactual and motivational obscenity of today. The former clearly implied a type of promiscuity, but it was organic, like the body's viscera, or again like objects piled up and accumulated in a private universe, or like all that is not spoken, teeming in the silence of repression. Unlike this organic, visceral, carnal promiscuity, the promiscuity that reigns over the communication networks is one of superficial saturation, of an incessant solicitation, of an extermination of interstitial and protective spaces. I pick up my telephone receiver and it's all there; the whole marginal network catches and harasses me with the insupportable good faith of everything that wants and claims to communicate. Free radio: it speaks, it sings, it expresses itself. Very well, *it* is the sympathetic obscenity of its content. In terms a little different for each medium, this is the result: a space, that of the FM band, is found to be saturated, the stations overlap and mix together (to the point that sometimes it no longer communicates at all). Something that was free by virtue of space is no longer. Speech is free perhaps, but I am less free than before: I no longer succeed in knowing what I want, the space is so saturated, the pressure so great from all who want to make themselves heard.

I fall into the negative ecstasy of the radio.

There is in effect a state of fascination and vertigo linked to this obscene delirium of communication. A singular form of pleasure perhaps, but aleatory and dizzying. If we follow Roger Caillois [7] in his classification of games (it's as good as any other) — games of expression (*mimicry*), games of competition (*agon*), games of chance (*alea*), games of vertigo (*ilynx*) — the whole tendency of our contemporary "culture" would lead us from a relative disappearance of forms of expression and competition (as we have remarked at the level of objects) to the advantages of forms of risk and vertigo. The latter no longer involve games of scene, mirror, challenge and duality; they are, rather, ecstatic, solitary and narcissistic. The pleasure is no longer one of manifestation, scenic and aesthetic, but rather one of pure fascination, aleatory and psychotropic. This is not necessarily a negative value judgment: here surely there is an original and profound mutation of the very forms of perception and pleasure. We are still measuring the consequences poorly. Wanting to apply our old criteria and the reflexes of a "scenic" sensibility, we no doubt misapprehend what may be the occurrence, in this sensory sphere, of something new, ecstatic and obscene.

One thing is sure: the scene excites us, the obscene fascinates us. With fascination and ecstasy, passion disappears. Investment, desire, passion, seduction or again, according to Caillois, expression and competition — the hot universe. Ecstasy, obscenity, fascination, communication or again, according to Caillois, hazard, chance and vertigo — the cold universe (even vertigo is cold, the psychedelic one of drugs in particular).

In any case, we will have to suffer this new state of things, this forced extroversion of all interiority, this forced injection of all exteriority that the categorical imperative of communication literally signifies. There also, one can perhaps make use of the old metaphors of pathology. If hysteria was the pathology of the exacerbated staging of the subject, a pathology of expression, of the body's theatrical and operatic conversion; and if paranoia was the pathology of organization, of the structuration of a rigid and jealous world; then with communication and information, with the immanent promiscuity of all these networks, with their continual connections, we are now in a new form of schizophrenia. No more hysteria, no more projective paranoia, properly speaking, but this state of terror proper to the schizophrenic: too great a proximity of everything, the unclean promiscuity of everything which touches, invests and penetrates without resistance, with no halo of private protection, not even his own body, to protect him anymore.

The schizo is bereft of every scene, open to everything in spite of himself, living in the greatest confusion. He is himself obscene, the obscene prey of the world's obscenity. What characterizes him is less the loss of the real, the light years of estrangement from the real, the pathos of distance and radical separation, as is commonly said: but, very much to the contrary, the absolute proximity, the total instantaneity of things, the feeling of no defense, no retreat. It is the end of interiority and intimacy, the overexposure and transparence of the world which traverses him without obstacle. He can no longer produce the limits of his own being, can no longer play nor stage himself, can no longer produce himself as mirror. He is now only a pure screen, a switching center for all the networks of influence.

Translated by John Johnston

References

1. *Le Système des objets* (Paris: Gallimard, 1968). [Tr.]
2. Baudrillard is alluding here to Marcel Mauss's theory of gift exchange and Georges Bataille's notion of *dépense*. The "accursed portion" in the latter's theory refers to whatever remains outside of society's rationalized economy of exchanges. See Bataille, *La Part Maudite* (Paris: Editions de Minuit, 1949). Baudrillard's own conception of symbolic exchange, as a form of interaction that lies outside of modern Western society and that therefore "haunts it like its own death," is developed in his *L'échange symbolique et la mort* (Paris: Gallimard, 1976). [Tr.]
3. See Roland Barthes, "The New Citroën," *Mythologies,* trans. Annette Lavers (New York: Hill and Wang, 1972), pp. 88-90. [Tr.]
4. Two observations. First, this is not due alone to the passage, as one wants to call it, from a society of abundance and surplus to a society of crisis and penury (economic reasons have never been worth very much). Just as the effect of consumption was not linked to the use value of things nor to their abundance, but precisely to the passage from use value to sign value, so here there is something new that is not linked to the end of abundance.
    Secondly, all this does not mean that the domestic universe—the home, its objects, etc.—is not still lived largely in a traditional way—social, psychological, differential, etc. It means rather that the stakes are no longer there, that another arrangement or life-style is virtually in place, even if it is indicated only through a technologistical discourse which is often simply a political gadget. But it is crucial to see that the analysis that one could make of objects and their system in the '60s and '70s essentially began with the language of advertising and the pseudo-conceptual discourse of the expert. "Consumption," the "strategy of desire," etc. were first only a metadiscourse, the analysis of a projective myth whose actual effect was never really known. How people actually live with their objects—at bottom, one knows no more about this than about the truth of primitive societies. That's why it is often problematic and useless to want to verify (statistically, objectively) these hypotheses, as one ought to be able to do as a good sociologist. As we know, the language of advertising is first for the use of the advertisers themselves. Nothing says that contemporary discourse on computer science and communication is not for the use alone of professionals in these fields. (As for the discourse of intellectuals and sociologists themselves . . .)

5. For an expanded explanation of this idea, see Baudrillard's essay "La précession des simulacres," *Simulacres et Simulation* (Paris: Galilée, 1981). An English translation appears in *Simulations* (New York: Foreign Agent Series, Semiotext(e) Publications, 1983). [Tr.]

6. A reference to Guy Debord's *La société du spectacle* (Paris: Buchet-Chastel, 1968). [Tr.]

7. Roger Caillois, *Les jeux et les hommes* (Paris: Gallimard, 1958). [Tr.]

Opponents, Audiences,
Constituencies and Community

EDWARD W. SAID

Who writes? For whom is the writing being done? In what circumstances? These, it seems to me, are the questions whose answers provide us with the ingredients making for a politics of interpretation. But if one does not wish to ask and answer the questions in a dishonest and abstract way, some attempt must be made to show why they are questions of some relevance to the present time. What needs to be said at the beginning is that the single most impressive aspect of the present time—at least for the "humanist," a description for which I have contradictory feelings of affection and revulsion—is that it is manifestly the Age of Ronald Reagan. And it is in this age as a context and setting that the politics of interpretation and the politics of culture are enacted.

I do not want to be misunderstood as saying that the cultural situation I describe here caused Reagan, or that it typifies Reaganism, or that everything about it can be ascribed or referred back to the personality of Ronald Reagan. What I argue is that a particular situation within the field we call "criticism" is not merely related to but is an integral part of the currents of thought and practice that play a role within the Reagan era. Moreover, I think, "criticism" and the traditional academic humanities have gone through a series of developments over time whose beneficiary and culmination is Reaganism. Those are the gross claims that I make for my argument.

A number of miscellaneous points need to be made here. I am fully aware that any effort to characterize the present cultural moment is very likely to seem quixotic at best, unprofessional at worst. But that, I submit, is an aspect of the present cultural moment, in which the social and historical setting of critical activity is a totality felt to be benign (free, apolitical,

This essay was originally published in *Critical Inquiry* 9 (September, 1982) and is reprinted here by permission of the author and University of Chicago Press.

serious), uncharacterizable as a whole (it is too complex to be described in general and tendentious terms) and somehow outside history. Thus it seems to me that one thing to be tried—out of sheer critical obstinacy—is precisely *that* kind of generalization, *that* kind of political portrayal, *that* kind of overview condemned by the present dominant culture to appear inappropriate and doomed from the start.

It is my conviction that culture works very effectively to make invisible and even "impossible" the actual *affiliations* that exist between the world of ideas and scholarship, on the one hand, and the world of brute politics, corporate and state power, and military force, on the other. The cult of expertise and professionalism, for example, has so restricted our scope of vision that a positive (as opposed to an implicit or passive) doctrine of noninterference among fields has set in. This doctrine has it that the general public is best left ignorant, and the most crucial policy questions affecting human existence are best left to "experts," specialists who talk about their specialty only, and—to use the word first given wide social approbation by Walter Lippmann in *Public Opinion* and *The Phantom Public*—"insiders," people (usually men) who are endowed with the special privilege of knowing how things really work and, more important, of being close to power.[1]

Humanistic culture in general has acted in tacit compliance with this antidemocratic view, the more regrettably since, both in their formulation and in the politics they have given rise to, so-called policy issues can hardly be said to enhance human community. In a world of increasing interdependence and political consciousness, it seems both violent and wasteful to accept the notion, for example, that countries ought to be classified simply as pro-Soviet or pro-American. Yet this classification—and with it the reappearance of a whole range of cold war motifs and symptoms (discussed by Noam Chomsky in *Towards a New Cold War*)—dominates thinking about foreign policy. There is little in humanistic culture that is an effective antidote to it, just as it is true that few humanists have very much to say about the problems starkly dramatized by the 1980 Report of the Independent Commission on International Development Issues, *North-South: A Programme for Survival*. Our political discourse is now choked with enormous, thought-stopping abstractions, from terrorism, Communism, Islamic fundamentalism, and instability, to moderation, freedom, stability and strategic alliances, all of them as unclear as they are both potent and unrefined in their appeal. It is next to impossible to think about human society either in a global way (as Richard Falk eloquently does in *A Global Approach to National Policy* [1975]) or at the level of everyday life. As Philip Green shows in *The Pursuit of Inequality,* notions like equality and welfare have simply been chased off the intellectual landscape. Instead a brutal Darwinian picture of self-help and self-promotion is proposed by Reaganism, both domestically and internationally, as an image of the world ruled by what is being called "productivity" or "free enterprise."

Add to this the fact that liberalism and the Left are in a state of intellectual disarray and fairly dismal perspectives emerge. The challenge posed by these perspectives is not how to cultivate one's garden despite them but how to understand cultural work occurring within them. What I propose here, then, is a rudimentary attempt to do just that, notwithstanding a good deal of inevitable incompleteness, overstatement, generalization, and crude characterization. Finally, I will very quickly propose an alternative way of undertaking cultural work, although anything like a fully worked-out program can only be done collectively and in a separate study.

My use of "constituency," "audience," "opponents" and "community" serves as a reminder that no one writes simply for oneself. There is always an Other; and this Other willy-nilly turns interpretation into a social activity, albeit with unforeseen consequences, audiences, constituencies and so on. And, I would add, interpretation is the work of intellectuals, a class badly in need today of moral rehabilitation and social redefinition. The one issue that urgently requires study is, for the humanist no less than for the social scientist, the status of *information* as a component of knowledge: its sociopolitical status, its contemporary fate, its economy (a subject treated recently by Herbert Schiller in *Who Knows: Information in the Age of the Fortune 500*). We all think we know what it means, for example, to *have* information and to write and interpret texts containing information. Yet we live in an age which places unprecedented emphasis on the production of knowledge and information, as Fritz Machlup's *Production and Distribution of Knowledge in the United States* dramatizes clearly. What happens to information and knowledge, then, when IBM and AT&T—two of the world's largest corporations—claim that what they do is put "knowledge" to work "for the people"? What is the role of humanistic knowledge and information if they are not to be unknowing (many ironies there) partners in commodity production and marketing, so much so that what humanists do may in the end turn out to be a quasi-religious concealment of this peculiarly unhumanistic process? A true secular politics of interpretation sidesteps this question at its peril.

At a recent MLA convention, I stopped by the exhibit of a major university press and remarked to the amiable sales representative on duty that there seemed to be no limit to the number of highly specialized books of advanced literary criticism his press put out. "Who reads these books?" I asked, implying of course that however brilliant and important most of them were they were difficult to read and therefore could not have a wide audience—or at least an audience wide enough to justify regular publication during a time of economic crisis. The answer I received made sense, assuming I was told the truth. People who write specialized, advanced (i.e., New New) criticism faithfully read each other's books. Thus each such book could be assured of, but wasn't necessarily always getting, sales of around three thousand copies, "all other things being equal." The last qualification struck me as ambiguous at best, but it needn't detain us here. The point was that a nice little audience had been built and could be routinely mined by this press; certainly, on a much larger scale, publishers of cookbooks and exercise manuals apply a related principle as they churn out what may seem like a very long series of unnecessary books, even if an expanding crowd of avid food and exercise aficionados is not quite the same thing as a steadily attentive and earnest crowd of three thousand critics reading each other.

What I find peculiarly interesting about the real or mythical three thousand is that whether they derive ultimately from the Anglo-American New Criticism (as formulated by I.A. Richards, William Empson, John Crowe Ransom, Cleanth Brooks, Allen Tate, and company, beginning in the 1920s and continuing for several decades thereafter) or from the so-called New New Criticism (Roland Barthes, Jacques Derrida, et al., during the 1960s), they vindicate, rather than undermine, the notion that intellectual labor ought to be divided into progressively narrower niches. Consider very quickly the irony of this. New Criticism claimed to view the verbal object as in itself it really was, free from the distractions of biography, social message, even paraphrase. Matthew Arnold's critical program was thereby to be advanced not by jumping directly from the text to the whole of culture but by using a highly concentrated verbal analysis to comprehend cultural values available only through a finely wrought literary structure finely understood.

Charges made against the American New Criticism that its ethos was clubby, gentlemanly or Episcopalian are, I think, correct only if it is added that in practice New Criticism, for all its elitism, was strangely populist in intention. The idea behind the pedagogy, and of course the preaching, of Brooks and Robert Penn Warren was that everyone properly instructed could feel, perhaps even act, like an educated gentleman. In its sheer projection this was by no means a trivial ambition. No amount of snide mocking at their gentility can conceal the fact that, in order to accomplish the conversion, the New Critics aimed at nothing less than the removal of *all* of what they considered the specialized rubbish—put there, they presumed, by professors of literature—standing between the reader of a poem and the poem. Leaving aside the questionable value of the New Criticism's ultimate social and moral message, we must concede that the school deliberately and perhaps incongruously tried to create a wide community of responsive readers out of a very large, potentially unlimited, constituency of students and teachers of literature.

In its early days, the French *nouvelle critique,* with Barthes as its chief apologist, attempted the same kind of thing. Once again the guild of professional literary scholars was characterized as impeding responsiveness to literature. Once again the antidote was what seemed to be a specialized reading technique based on a near jargon of linguistic, psychoanalytic and Marxist terms, all of which proposed a new freedom for writers and literate readers alike. The philosophy of *écriture* promised wider horizons and a less restricted community, once an initial (and as it turned out painless) surrender to structuralist activity had been made. For despite structuralist prose, there was no impulse among the principal structuralists to exclude readers; quite the contrary, as Barthes's often abusive attacks on Raymond Picard show, the main purpose of critical reading was to create new readers of the classics who might otherwise have been frightened off by their lack of professional literary accreditation.

For about four decades, then, in both France and the United States, the schools of "new" critics were committed to prying literature and writing loose from confining institutions. However much it was to depend upon carefully learned technical skills, reading was in very large measure to become an act of public depossession. Texts were to be unlocked or decoded, then handed on to anyone who was interested. The resources of symbolic language were placed at the disposal of readers who it was assumed suffered the debilitations of either irrelevant "professional" information or the accumulated habits of lazy inattention.

Thus French and American New Criticism were, I believe, competitors for authority within mass culture, not other-worldly alternatives to it. Because of what became of them, we have tended to forget the original missionary aims the two schools set for themselves. They belong to precisely the same moment that produced Jean-Paul Sartre's ideas about an engaged literature and a committed writer. Literature was about the world, readers were in the world; the question was not *whether* to be but *how* to be, and this was best answered by carefully analyzing language's symbolic enactments of the various existential possibilities available to human beings. What the Franco-American critics shared was the notion that verbal discipline could be self-sufficient once you learned to think pertinently about language stripped of unnecessary scaffolding; in other words, you did not need to be a professor to benefit from Donne's metaphors or Saussure's liberating distinction between *langue* and *parole*. And so the New Criticism's precious and cliquish aspect was mitigated by its radically anti-institutional bias, which manifested itself in the enthusiastic therapeutic optimism to be observed in both France and the United States. Join humankind against the schools: this was a message a great many people could appreciate.

How strangely perverse, then, that the legacy of both types of New Criticism is the private-clique consciousness embodied in a kind of critical writing that has virtually abandoned any attempt at reaching a large, if not a mass, audience. My belief is that both in the United States and in France the tendency toward formalism in New Criticism was accentuated by the academy. For the fact is that a disciplined attention to language can only thrive in the rarefied atmosphere of the classroom. Linguistics and literary analysis are features of the modern school, not of the marketplace. Purifying the language of the tribe—whether as a project subsumed within modernism or as a hope kept alive by embattled New Criticisms surrounded by mass culture—always moved further from the really big existing tribes and closer toward emerging new ones, comprised of the acolytes of a reforming or even revolutionary creed who in the end seemed to care more about turning the new creed into an intensely separatist orthodoxy than about forming a large community of readers.

To its unending credit, the university protects such wishes and shelters them under the umbrella of academic freedom. Yet advocacy of *close reading* or of *écriture* can quite naturally entail hostility to outsiders who fail to grasp the salutary powers of verbal analysis; moreover, persuasion too often has turned out to be less important than purity of intention and execution. In time the guild adversarial sense grew as the elaborate techniques multiplied, and an interest in expanding the constituency lost out to a wish for abstract correctness and methodological rigor within a quasi-monastic order. Critics read each other and cared about little else.

The parallels between the fate of a New Criticism reduced to abandoning universal literacy entirely and that of the school of F.R. Leavis are sobering. As Francis Mulhern reminds us in *The Moment of Scrutiny,* Leavis was not a formalist himself and began his career in the context of generally Left politics. Leavis argued that great literature was fundamentally opposed to a class society and to the dictates of a coterie. In his view, English studies ought to become the cornerstone of a new, fundamentally democratic outlook. But largely because the Leavisites concentrated their work both in and for the university, what began as a healthy oppositional participation in modern industrial society changed into a shrill withdrawal from it. English studies became narrower and narrower, in my opinion, and critical reading degenerated into decisions about what should or should not be allowed into the great tradition.

I do not want to be misunderstood as saying that there is something inherently pernicious about the modern university that produces the changes I have been describing. Certainly there is a great deal to be said in favor of a university manifestly not influenced or controlled by coarse partisan politics. But one thing in particular about the university—and here I speak about the modern university without distinguishing between European, American, or Third World and socialist universities—does appear to exercise an almost totally unrestrained influence: the principle that knowledge ought to exist, be sought after and disseminated in a very divided form. Whatever the social, political, economic and ideological reasons underlying this principle, it has not long gone without its challengers. Indeed, it may not be too much of an exaggeration to say that one of the most interesting motifs in modern world culture has been the debate between proponents of the belief that knowledge can exist in a synthetic universal form and, on the other hand, those who believe that knowledge is inevitably produced and nurtured in specialized compartments. Georg Lukács's attack on reification and his advocacy of "totality," in my opinion, very tantalizingly resemble the wide-ranging discussions that have been taking place in the Islamic world since the late nineteenth century on the need for mediating between the claims of a totalizing Islamic vision and modern specialized science. These epistemological controversies are therefore centrally important to the workplace of knowledge production, the university, in which *what* knowledge is and how it ought to be discovered are the very lifeblood of its being.

The most impressive recent work concerning the history, circumstances and constitution of modern knowledge has stressed the role of social convention. Thomas Kuhn's "paradigm of research," for example, shifts attention away from the individual creator to the communal restraints upon personal initiative. Galileos and Einsteins are infrequent figures not just because genius is a rare thing but because scientists are borne along by agreed-upon ways to do research, and this consensus encourages uniformity rather than bold enterprise. Over time this uniformity acquires the status of a discipline, while its subject matter becomes a field or territory. Along with these goes a whole apparatus of techniques, one of whose functions is, as Michel Foucault has tried to show in *The Archaeology of Knowledge*, to protect the coherence, the territorial integrity, the social identity of the field, its adherents and its institutional presence. You cannot simply choose to be a sociologist or a psychoanalyst; you cannot simply make statements that have the status of knowledge in anthropology; you cannot merely suppose that what you say as a historian (however well it may have been researched) enters historical discourse. You have to pass through certain rules of accreditation, you must learn the rules, you must speak the language, you must master the idioms and you must accept the authorities of the field — determined in many of the same ways — to which you want to contribute.

In this view of things, expertise is partially determined by how well an individual learns the rules of the game, so to speak. Yet it is difficult to determine in absolute terms whether expertise is *mainly* constituted by the social conventions governing the intellectual manners of scientists or, on the other hand, mainly by the putative exigencies of the subject matter itself. Certainly convention, tradition and habit create ways of looking at a subject that transform it completely; and just as certainly there are generic differences between the subjects of history, literature and philology that require different (albeit related) techniques of analysis, disciplinary attitudes and commonly held views. Elsewhere I have taken the admittedly aggressive position that Orientalists, area-studies experts, journalists and foreign-policy specialists are not always sensitive to the dangers of self-quotation, endless repetition, and received ideas that their fields encourage, for reasons that have more to do with politics and ideology than with any "outside" reality. Hayden White has shown in his work that historians are subject not just to narrative conventions but also to the virtually closed space imposed on the interpreter of events by verbal retrospection, which is very far from being an objective mirror of reality. Yet even these views, although they are understandably repugnant to many people, do not go as far as saying that everything about a "field" can be reduced either to an interpretive convention or to political interest.

Let us grant, therefore, that it would be a long and potentially impossible task to prove empirically that, on the one hand, there could be objectivity so far as knowledge about human society is concerned or, on the other, that all knowledge is esoteric and subjective. Much ink has been spilled on both sides of the debate, not all of it useful, as Wayne Booth has shown in his discussion of scientism and modernism, *Modern Dogma and the Rhetoric of Assent*. An instructive opening out of the impasse—to which I want to return a bit later—has been the body of techniques developed by the school of reader-response critics: Wolfgang Iser, Norman Holland, Stanley Fish, and Michael Riffaterre, among others. These critics argue that since texts without readers are no less incomplete than readers without texts, we should focus attention on what happens when both components of the interpretive situation interact. Yet with the exception of Fish, reader-response critics tend to regard interpretation as an essentially private, interiorized happening, thereby inflating the role of solitary decoding at the expense of its just as important social context. In his latest book, *Is There a Text in This Class?*, Fish accentuates the role of what he calls interpretive communities, groups as well as institutions (principal among them the classroom and predagogues) whose presence, much more than any unchanging objective standard or correlative of absolute truth, controls what we consider to be knowledge. If, as he says, "interpretation is the only game in town," then it must follow that interpreters who work mainly by persuasion and not scientific demonstration are the only players.

I am on Fish's side there. Unfortunately, though, he does not go very far in showing why, or even how, some interpretations are more persuasive than others. Once again we are back to the quandary suggested by the three thousand advanced critics reading each other to everyone else's unconcern. Is it the inevitable conclusion to the formation of an interpretive community that its constituency, its specialized language and its concerns tend to get tighter, more airtight, more self-enclosed as its own self-confirming authority acquires more power, the solid status of orthodoxy and a stable constituency? What is the acceptable humanistic antidote to what one discovers, say among sociologists, philosophers and so-called policy scientists who speak only to and for each other in a language oblivious to everything but a well-guarded, constantly shrinking fiefdom forbidden to the uninitiated?

For all sorts of reasons, large answers to these questions do not strike me as attractive or convincing. For one, the universalizing habit by which a system of thought is believed to account for everything too quickly slides into a quasi-religious synthesis. This, it seems to me, is the sobering lesson offered by John Fekete in *The Critical Twilight,* an account of how New Criticism led directly to Marshall McLuhan's "technocratic-religious eschatology." In fact, interpretation and its demands add up to a rough game, once we allow ourselves to step out of the shelter offered by specialized fields and by fancy all-embracing mythologies. The trouble with visions, reductive answers and systems is that they homogenize evidence very easily. Criticism as such is crowded out and disallowed from the start, hence impossible; and in the end one learns to manipulate bits of the system like so many parts of a machine. Far from taking in a great deal, the universal system as a universal type of explanation either screens out everything it cannot directly absorb or it repetitively churns out the same sort of thing all the time. In this way it becomes a kind of conspiracy theory. Indeed, it has always seemed to me that the supreme irony of what Derrida has called logocentrism is that its critique, deconstruction, is as insistent, as monotonous and as inadvertently systematizing as logocentrism itself. We may applaud the wish to break out of departmental divisions, therefore, without at the same time accepting the notion that one single method for doing so exists. The unheeding insistence of René Girard's "interdisciplinary" studies of mimetic desire and scapegoat effects is that they want to convert all human activity, all disciplines, to one thing. How can we assume this one thing covers everything that is essential, as Girard keeps suggesting?

This is only a relative skepticism, for one can prefer foxes to hedgehogs without also saying that all foxes are equal. Let us venture a couple of crucial distinctions. To the ideas of Kuhn, Foucault and Fish we can usefully add those of Giovanni Battista Vico and Antonio Gramsci. Here is what we come up with. Discourses, interpretive communities and paradigms of research are produced by intellectuals, Gramsci says, who can either be religious or secular. Now Gramsci's implicit contrast of secular with religious intellectuals is less familiar than his celebrated division between organic and traditional intellectuals. Yet it is no less important for that matter. In a letter of 17 August 1931, Gramsci writes about an old teacher from his Cagliari days, Umberto Cosmo:

It seemed to me that I and Cosmo, and many other intellectuals at this time (say the first fifteen years of the century) occupied a certain common ground: we were all to some degree part of the movement of moral and intellectual reform which in Italy stemmed from Benedetto Croce, and whose first premise was that modern man can and should live without the help of religion... positivist religion, mythological religion, or whatever brand one cares to name....[2] This point appears to me even today to be the major contribution made to international culture by modern Italian intellectuals, and it seems to me a civil conquest that must not be lost.[3]

Benedetto Croce of course was Vico's greatest modern student, and it was one of Croce's intentions in writing about Vico to reveal explicitly the strong secular bases of his thought and also to argue in favor of a secure and dominant civil culture (hence Gramsci's use of the phrase "civil conquest"). "Conquest" has perhaps a strange inappropriateness to it, but it serves to dramatize Gramsci's contention—also implicit in Vico—that the modern European state is possible not only because there is a political apparatus (army, police force, bureaucracy) but because there is a civil, secular and nonecclesiastical society making the state possible, providing the state with something to rule, filling the state with its humanly generated economic, cultural, social and intellectual production.

Gramsci was unwilling to let the Vichian-Crocean achievement of civil society's secular working go in the direction of what he called "immanentist thought." Like Arnold before him, Gramsci understood that if nothing in the social world is natural, not even nature, then it must also be true that things exist not only because they come into being and are created by human agency (*nascimento*) but also because by coming into being they displace something else that is already there: this is the combative and emergent aspect of social change as it applies to the world of culture linked to social history. To adapt from a statement Gramsci makes in *The Modern Prince,* "reality (and hence cultural reality) is a product of the application of human will to the society of things," and since also "everything is political, even philosophy and philosophies," we are to understand that in the realm of culture and of thought each production exists not only to earn a place for itself but to displace, win out over, others.[4] All ideas, philosophies, views and texts aspire to the consent of their consumers, and here Gramsci is more percipient than most in recognizing that there is a set of characteristics unique to civil society in which texts—embodying ideas, philosophies and so forth—acquire power through what Gramsci describes as diffusion, dissemination into and hegemony over the world of "common sense." Thus ideas aspire to the condition of acceptance; which is to say that one can interpret the meaning of a text by virtue of what in its mode of social presence enables its consent by either a small or a wide group of people.

The secular intellectuals are implicitly present at the center of these considerations. Social and intellectual authority for them does not derive directly from the divine but from an analyzable history made by human beings. Here Vico's counterposing of the sacred with what he calls the gentile realm is essential. Created by God, the sacred is a realm accessible only through revelation: it is ahistorical because complete and divinely untouchable. But whereas Vico has little interest in the divine, the gentile world obsesses him. "Gentile" derives from *gens,* the family group whose exfoliation in time generates history. But "gentile" is also a secular expanse because the web of filiations and affiliations that composes human history —law, politics, literature, power, science, emotion—is informed by *ingegno,* human ingenuity and spirit. This, and not a divine *fons et origo,* is accessible to Vico's new science.

But here a very particular kind of secular interpretation and, even more interestingly, a very particular conception of the interpretive situation is entailed. A direct index of this is the confusing organization of Vico's book, which seems to move sideways and backward as often as it moves forward. Because in a very precise sense God has been excluded from Vico's secular history, that history, as well as everything within it, presents its interpreter with a vast horizontal expanse, across which are to be seen many interrelated structures. The verb "to look" is therefore frequently employed by Vico to suggest what historical interpreters need to do. What one cannot see or look at—the past, for example—is to be divined; Vico's irony is too clear to miss, since what he argues is that only by putting oneself in the position of the maker (or divinity) can one grasp how the past has shaped the present. This involves speculation, supposition, imagination, sympathy; but in no instance can it be allowed that something other than human agency caused history. To be sure, there are historical laws of development, just as there is something that Vico calls divine Providence mysteriously at work inside history. The fundamental thing is that history and human society are made up of numerous efforts crisscrossing each other, frequently at odds with each other, always untidy in the way they involve each other. Vico's writing directly reflects this crowded spectacle.

One last observation needs to be made. For Gramsci and Vico, interpretation must take account of this secular horizontal space only by means appropriate to what is present there. I understand this to imply that no single explanation sending one back immediately to a single origin is adequate. And just as there are no simple dynastic answers, there are no simple discrete historical formations or social processes. A heterogeneity of human involvement is therefore equivalent to a heterogeneity of results, as well as of interpretive skills and techniques. There is no center, no inertly given and accepted authority, no fixed barriers ordering human history, even though authority, order and distinction exist. The secular intellectual works to show the absence of divine originality and, on the other side, the complex presence of historical actuality. The conversion of the absence of religion into the presence of actuality is secular interpretation.

Having rejected global and falsely systematic answers, one had better speak in a limited and concrete way about the contemporary actuality, which so far as our discussion here is concerned is Reagan's America, or, rather, the America inherited and now ruled over by Reaganism. Take literature and politics, for example. It is not too much of an exaggeration to say that an implicit consensus has been building for the past decade in which the study of literature is considered to be profoundly, even constitutively nonpolitical. When you discuss Keats or Shakespeare or Dickens, you may touch on political subjects, of course, but it is assumed that the skills traditionally associated with modern literary criticism (what is now called rhetoric, reading, textuality, tropology or deconstruction) are there to be applied to *literary* texts, not, for instance, to a government document, a sociological or ethnological report or a newspaper. This separation of fields, objects, disciplines and foci constitutes an amazingly *rigid* structure which, to my knowledge, is almost never discussed by literary scholars. There seems to be an unconsciously held norm guaranteeing the simple essence of "fields," a word which in turn has acquired the intellectual authority of a natural, objective fact. Separation, simplicity, silent norms of pertinence: this is one depoliticizing strain of considerable force, since it is capitalized on by professions, institutions, discourses and a massively reinforced consistency of specialized fields. One corollary of this is the proliferating orthodoxy of separate fields. "I'm sorry I can't understand this—I'm a literary critic, not a sociologist."

The intellectual toll this has taken in the work of the most explicitly political of recent critics—Marxists, in the instance I shall discuss here—is very high. Fredric Jameson has recently produced what is by any standard a major work of intellectual criticism, *The Political Unconscious*. What it discusses, it discusses with a rare brilliance and learning: I have no reservations at all about that. He argues that priority ought to be given to the political interpretation of literary texts and that Marxism, as an interpretive act as opposed to other methods, is "that 'untranscendable horizon' that subsumes such apparently antagonistic or incommensurable critical operations [as the other varieties of interpretive act] assigning them an undoubted sectoral validity within itself, and thus at once cancelling and preserving them." [5] Thus Jameson avails himself of all the most powerful and contradictory of contemporary methodologies, enfolding them in a series of original readings of modern novels, producing in the end a working through of three "semantic horizons" of which the third "phase" is the Marxist: hence, from *explica-*

tion de texte, through the ideological discourses of social classes, to the ideology of form itself, perceived against the ultimate horizon of human history.

It cannot be emphasized too strongly that Jameson's book presents a remarkably complex and deeply attractive argument to which I cannot do justice here. This argument reaches its climax in Jameson's conclusion, in which the utopian element in all cultural production is shown to play an underanalyzed and liberating role in human society; additionally, in a much too brief and suggestive passage, Jameson touches on three political discussions (involving the state, law and nationalism) for which the Marxist hermeneutic he has outlined, fully a negative as well as a positive hermeneutic, can be particularly useful.

We are still left, however, with a number of nagging difficulties. Beneath the surface of the book lies an unadmitted dichotomy between two kinds of "Politics": (1) the politics defined by political theory from Hegel to Louis Althusser and Ernst Bloch; (2) the politics of struggle and power in the everyday world, which in the United States at least has been won, so to speak, by Reagan. As to why this distinction should exist at all, Jameson says very little. This is even more troubling when we realize that Politics 2 is only discussed once, in the course of a long footnote. There he speaks in a general way about "ethnic groups, neighborhood movements, . . . rank and file labor groups," and so on and quite perspicaciously enters a plea for alliance politics in the United States as distinguished from France, where the totalizing global politics imposed on nearly every constituency has either inhibited or repressed their local development (p. 54). He is absolutely right of course (and would have been more so had he extended his arguments to a United States dominated by only two parties). Yet the irony is that in criticizing the global perspective and admitting its radical discontinuity with local alliance politics, Jameson is also advocating a strong hermeneutic globalism which will have the effect of subsuming the local in the synchronic. This is almost like saying: Don't worry; Reagan is merely a passing phenomenon: the cunning of history will get him too. Yet except for what suspiciously resembles a religious confidence in the teleological efficacy of the Marxist vision, there is no way, to my mind, by which the local is necessarily going to be subsumed, cancelled, preserved and resolved by the synchronic. Moreover, Jameson leaves it entirely up to the reader to guess what the connection is between the synchrony and theory of Politics 1 and the molecular struggles of Politics 2. Is there continuity or discontinuity between one realm and the other? How do quotidian politics and the struggle for power enter into the hermeneutic, if not by simple instruction from above or by passive osmosis?

These are unanswered questions precisely because, I think, Jameson's assumed constituency is an audience of cultural-literary critics. And this constituency in contemporary America is premised on and made possible by the separation of disciplines I spoke about earlier. This further aggravates the discursive separation of Politics 1 from Politics 2, creating the obvious impression that Jameson is dealing with autonomous realms of human effort. And this has a still more paradoxical result. In his concluding chapter, Jameson suggests allusively that the components of class consciousness — such things as group solidarity against outside threats — are at bottom utopian "insofar as all such (class-based) collectivities are *figures* for the ultimate concrete collective life of an achieved Utopian or classless society." Right at the heart of this thesis we find the notion that "ideological commitment is not first and foremost a matter of moral choice but of the taking of sides in a struggle between embattled groups" (290, 291). The difficulty here is that whereas moral choice is a category to be rigorously de-Platonized and historicized, there is no inevitability — logical or otherwise — for reducing it completely to "the taking of sides in a struggle between embattled groups." On the molecular level of an individual peasant family thrown off its land, who is to say whether the desire for restitution is exclusively a matter of taking sides or of making the moral choice to resist dispossession? I cannot be sure. But what is so indicative of Jameson's position is that from the global, synchronic hermeneutic overview, moral choice plays no role, and, what is more, the matter is not investigated empirically or historically (as Barrington Moore has tried to do in *Injustice: The Social Basis of Obedience and Revolt*).

Jameson has certainly earned the right to be one of the preeminent spokesmen for what is best in American cultural Marxism. He is discussed this way by a well-known English Marxist, Terry Eagleton, in a recent article, "The Idealism of American Criticism." Eagleton's discussion contrasts Jameson and Frank Lentricchia with the main currents of contemporary American theory which, according to Eagleton, "develops by way of inventing new idealist devices for the repression of history."[6] Nevertheless, Eagleton's admiration for Jameson and Lentricchia does not prevent him from seeing the limitations of their work, their political "unclarity," their lingering pragmatism, eclecticism, the relationship of their hermeneutic criticism to Reagan's ascendancy and — in Jameson's case especially — their nostalgic Hegelianism. This is not to say, however, that Eagleton expects either of them to toe the current ultra-Left line, which alleges that "the production of Marxist readings of classical texts is class-collaborationism." But he is right to say that "the question irresistibly raised for the Marxist reader of Jameson is simply this: How is a Marxist-structuralist analysis of a minor novel of Balzac to help shake the foundations of capitalism?" Clearly the answer to this question is that such readings won't; but what does Eagleton propose as an alternative? Here we come to the disabling cost of rigidly enforced intellectual and disciplinary divisions, which also affects Marxism.

For we may as well acknowledge that Eagleton writes about Jameson as a fellow Marxist. This is intellectual solidarity, yes, but within a "field" defined principally as an intellectual discourse existing solely within an academy that has left the extra-academic outside world to the new Right and to Reagan. It follows with a kind of natural inevitability that if one such confinement is acceptable, others can be acceptable: Eagleton faults Jameson for the practical ineffectiveness of his Marxist-structuralism but, on the other hand, meekly takes for granted that he and Jameson inhabit the small world of literary studies, speak its language, deal only with its problematics. Why this should be so is hinted at obscurely by Eagleton when he avers that "the ruling class" determines what uses are made of literature for the purpose of "ideological reproduction" and that as revolutionaries "we" cannot select "the literary terrain on which the battle is to be engaged." It does not seem to have occurred to Eagleton that what he finds weakest in Jameson and Lentricchia, their marginality and vestigial idealism, is what also makes him bewail their rarefied discourse at the same time that he somehow accepts it as his own. The very same specialized ethos has been attenuated a little more now: Eagleton, Jameson and Lentricchia are literary Marxists who write for literary Marxists, who are in cloistral seclusion from the inhospitable world of real politics. Both "literature" and "Marxism" are thereby confirmed in their apolitical content and methodology: literary criticism is still "only" literary criticism, Marxism only Marxism, and politics is mainly what the literary critic talks about longingly and hopelessly.

This rather long digression on the consequences of the separation of "fields" brings me directly to a second aspect of the politics of interpretation viewed from a secular perspective rigorously responsive to the Age of Reagan. It is patently true that, even within the atomized order of disciplines and fields, methodological investigations can and indeed do occur. But the prevailing mode of intellectual discourse is militantly antimethodological, if by methodological we mean a questioning of the structure of fields and discourses themselves. A principle of silent exclusion operates within and at the boundaries of discourse; this has now become so internalized that fields, disciplines and their discourses have taken on the status of immutable durability. Licensed members of the field, which has all the trappings of a social institution, are identifiable as belonging to a guild, and for them words like "expert" and "objective" have an important resonance. To acquire a position of authority within the field is, however, to be involved internally in the formation of a canon, which usually turns out to be a blocking device for methodological and disciplinary self-questioning. When J. Hillis Miller says, "I believe in the established canon of English and American Literature and the validity of the concept of privileged texts," he is saying something that has moment by virtue neither of its logical truth nor of its demonstrable clarity.[7] Its power derives from his social authority as a well-known professor of English, a man of deservedly great reputation, a teacher of well-placed students. And what he says more or less eliminates the possibility of asking whether canons (and the imprimatur placed upon canons by a literary circle) are more methodologically necessary to the order of dominance within a guild than they are to the secular study of human history.

If I single out literary and humanistic scholars in what I am saying, it is because, for better or worse, I am dealing with texts, and texts are the very point of departure and culmination for literary scholars. Literary scholars read and they write, both of which are activities having more to do with wit, flexibility and questioning than they do with solidifying ideas into institutions or with bludgeoning readers into unquestioning submission. Above all it seems to me that it goes directly against the grain of reading and writing to erect barriers between texts or to create monuments out of texts—unless, of course, literary scholars believe themselves to be servants of some outside power requiring this duty from them. The curricula of most literature departments in the university today are constructed almost entirely out of monuments, canonized into rigid dynastic formation, serviced and reserviced monotonously by a shrinking guild of humble servitors. The irony is that this is usually done in the name of historical research and traditional humanism, and yet such canons often have very little historical accuracy to them. To take one small example, Robert Darnton has shown that

> much of what passes today as 18th century French literature wasn't much read by Frenchman in the 18th century. . . . We suffer from an arbitrary notion of literary history as a canon of classics, one which was developed by professors of literature in the 19th and 20th centuries—while in fact what people of the 18th century were reading was very different. By studying the publisher's accounts and papers at [the Société Typographique de] Neufchatel I've been able to construct a kind of bestseller list of pre-revolutionary France, and it doesn't look anything like the reading lists passed out in classrooms today.[8]

Hidden beneath the pieties surrounding the canonical monuments is a guild solidarity that dangerously resembles a religious consciousness. It is worth recalling Michael Bakunin in *Dieu et l'état:* "In their existing organization, monopolizing science and remaining thus outside social life, the *savants* form a separate caste, in many respects analogous to the priesthood. Scientific abstraction is their God, living and real individuals are their victims, and they are the consecrated and licensed sacrificers." [9] The current interest in producing enormous biographies of consecrated great authors is one aspect of this priestifying. By isolating and elevating the subject beyond his or her time and society, an exaggerated respect for single individuals is produced along with, naturally enough, awe for the biographer's craft. There are similar distortions in the emphasis placed on autobiographical literature whose modish name is "self-fashioning."

All this, then, atomizes, privatizes and reifies the untidy realm of secular history and creates a peculiar configuration of constituencies and interpretive communities: this is the third major aspect of a contemporary politics of interpretation. An almost invariable rule of order is that very little of the *circumstances* making interpretive activity possible is allowed to seep into the interpretive circle itself. This is peculiarly (not to say distressingly) in evidence when humanists are called in to dignify discussions of major public issues. I shall say nothing here about the egregious lapses (mostly concerning the relationship between the government-corporate policymakers and humanists on questions of national and foreign policy) to be found in the Rockefeller Foundation-funded report *The Humanities in American Life.* More crudely dramatic for my purposes is another Rockefeller enterprise, a conference on "The Reporting of Religion in the Media," held in August 1980. In addressing his opening remarks to the assembled collection of clerics, philosophers and other humanists, Martin Marty evidently felt it would be elevating the discussion somewhat if he brought Admiral Stansfield Turner, head of the CIA, to his assistance: he therefore "quoted Admiral Turner's assertion that United States intelligence agencies had overlooked the importance of religion in Iran, 'because everyone knew it had so little place and power in the modern world.'" No one seemed to notice the natural affinity assumed by Marty between the CIA and scholars. It was all part of the mentality decreeing that humanists were humanists and experts experts no matter who sponsored their work, usurped their freedom of judgment and independence of research or assimilated them unquestioningly to state service, even as they protested again and again that they were objective and nonpolitical.

Let me cite one small personal anecdote at the risk of overstating the point. Shortly before my book *Covering Islam* appeared, a private foundation convened a seminar on the book to be attended by journalists, scholars and diplomats, all of whom had professional interests in how the Islamic world was being reported and represented in the West generally. I was to answer questions. One Pulitzer Prize-winning journalist, who is now the foreign news editor of a leading Eastern newspaper, was asked to lead the discussion, which he did by summarizing my argument briefly and on the whole not very accurately. He concluded his remarks by a question meant to initiate discussion: "Since you say that Islam is badly reported [actually my argument in the book is that "Islam" isn't something to be reported or nonreported: it is an ideological abstraction], could you tell us how we should report the Islamic world in order to help clarify the U.S.'s strategic interests there?" When I objected to the question, on the grounds that journalism was supposed to be either reporting or analyzing the news and not serving as an adjunct to the National Security Council, no attention was paid to what in everyone's eyes was an irrelevant naiveté on my part. Thus have the security interests of the state been absorbed silently into journalistic interpretation: expertise is therefore supposed to be unaffected by its institutional affiliations with power, although of course it is exactly those affiliations — hidden but assumed unquestioningly — that make the expertise possible and imperative.

Given this context, then, a constituency is principally a clientele: people who use (and perhaps buy) your services because you and others belonging to your guild are certified experts. For the relatively unmarketable humanists whose wares are "soft" and whose expertise is almost by definition marginal, their constituency is a fixed one composed of other humanists, students, government and corporate executives and media employees, who use the humanist to assure a harmless place for "the humanities" or culture or literature in the society. I hasten to recall, however, that this is the role voluntarily accepted by humanists whose notion of what they do is neutralized, specialized and nonpolitical in the extreme. To an alarming degree, the present continuation of the humanities depends, I think, on the sustained self-purification of humanists for whom the ethic of specialization has become equivalent to minimizing the content of their work and increasing the composite wall of guild consciousness, social authority and exclusionary discipline around themselves. Opponents are therefore not people in disagreement with the constituency but people to be kept out, nonexperts and nonspecialists, for the most part.

Whether all this makes an interpretive *community*, in the secular and noncommercial, noncoercive sense of the word, is very seriously to be doubted. If a community is based principally on keeping people out and on defending a tiny fiefdom (in perfect complicity with the defenders of other fiefdoms) on the basis of a mysteriously pure subject's inviolable integrity, then it is a religious community. The secular realm I have presupposed requires a more open sense of community as something to be won and of audiences as human beings to be addressed. How, then, can we understand the present setting in such a way as to see in it the possibility of change? How can interpretation be interpreted as having a secular, political force in an age determined to deny interpretation anything but a role as mystification?

I shall organize my remarks around the notion of *representation,* which, for literary scholars at least, has a primordial importance. From Aristotle to Auerbach and after, mimesis is inevitably to be found in discussions of literary texts. Yet as even Auerbach himself showed in his monographic stylistic studies, techniques of representation in literary work have always been related to, and in some measure have depended on, social formations. The phrase "la cour et la ville," for example, makes primarily *literary* sense in a text by Nicolas Boileau, and although the text itself gives the phrase a peculiarly refined local meaning, it nevertheless presupposed both an audience that knew he referred to what Auerbach calls "his social environment" and the social environment itself, which made references to it possible. This is not *simply* a matter of reference, since, from a verbal point of view, referents can be said to be equal and equally verbal. Even in very minute analyses, Auerbach's view does, however, have to do with the *coexistence* of realms—the literary, the social, the personal—and the way in which they make use of, affiliate with and represent each other.

With very few exceptions, contemporary literary theories assume the relative independence and even autonomy of literary representation over (and not just from) all others. Novelistic verisimilitude, poetic tropes and dramatic metaphors (Lukács, Harold Bloom, Francis Ferguson) are representations to and for themselves of the novel, the poem, the drama: this, I think, accurately sums up the assumptions underlying the three influential (and, in their own way, typical) theories I have referred to. Moreover, the organized study of literature—*en soi* and *pour soi*—is premised on the constitutively primary act of literary (that is, artistic) representation, which in turn absorbs and incorporates other realms, other representations, secondary to it. But all this institutional weight has precluded a sustained, systematic examination of the coexistence of and the interrelationship between the literary and the social, which is where representation—from journalism, to political struggle, to economic production and power—plays an extraordinarily important role. Confined to the study of one representational complex, literary critics accept and paradoxically ignore the lines drawn around what they do.

This is depoliticization with a vengeance, and it must, I think, be understood as an integral part of the historical moment presided over by Reaganism. The division of intellectual labor I spoke of earlier can now be seen as assuming a *thematic* importance in the contemporary culture as a whole. For if the study of literature is "only" about literary representation, then it must be the case that literary representations and literary activities (writing, reading, producing the "humanities," and arts and letters) are essentially ornamental, possessing at most secondary ideological characteristics. The consequence is that to deal with literature as well as the broadly defined "humanities" is to deal with the nonpolitical, although quite evidently the political realm is presumed to lie just beyond (and beyond the reach of) literary, and hence *literate,* concern.

A perfect recent embodiment of this state of affairs is the 30 September 1981 issue of *The New Republic.* The lead editorial analyzes the United States's policy toward South Africa and ends up supporting this policy, which even the most "moderate" of Black African states interpret (correctly, as even the United States explicitly confesses) as a policy supporting the South African settler-colonial regime. The last article of the issue includes a mean personal attack on me as "an intellectual in the thrall of Soviet totalitarianism," a claim that is as disgustingly McCarthyite as it is intellectually fraudulent. Now at the very center of this issue of the magazine—a fairly typical issue by the way—is a long and decently earnest book review by Christopher Hill, a leading Marxist historian. What boggles the mind is not the mere coincidence of apologies for apartheid rubbing shoulders with good Marxist sense but how the one antipode includes (without any reference at all) what the other, the Marxist pole, performs unknowingly.

There are two very impressive points of reference for this discussion of what can be called the national culture as a nexus of relationships between "fields," many of them employing representation as their technique of distribution and production. (It will be obvious here that I exclude the creative arts and the natural sciences.) One is Perry Anderson's "Components of the National Culture" (1969);[10] the other is Regis Debray's study of the French intelligentsia, *Teachers, Writers, Celebrities* (1980). Anderson's argument is that an absent intellectual center in traditional British thought about society was vulnerable to a "white" (antirevolutionary, conservative) immigration into Britain from Europe. This in turn produced a blockage of sociology, a technicalization of philosophy, an idea-free empiricism in history and an idealist aesthetics. Together these and other disciplines form "something like a closed system," in which subversive discourses like Marxism and psychoanalysis were for a time quarantined; now, however, they too have been incorporated. The French case, according to Debray, exhibits a series of three hegemonic conquests in time. First there was the era of the secular universities, which ended with World War I. That was succeeded by the era of the publishing houses, a time between the wars when Galimard-NRF—agglomerates of gifted writers and essayists that included Jacques Rivière, André Gide, Marcel Proust and Paul Valéry—replaced the social and intellectual authority of the somewhat overproductive, masspopulated universities. Finally, during the 1960s, intellectual life was absorbed into the structure of the mass media: worth, merit, attention and visibility slipped from the pages of books to be estimated by frequency of appearance on the television screen. At this point, then, a new hierarchy, what Debray calls a mediocracy, emerges, and it rules the schools and the book industry.

There are certain similarities between Debray's France and Anderson's England, on the one hand, and Reagan's America, on the other. They are interesting, but I cannot spend time talking about them. The differences are, however, more instructive. Unlike France, high culture in America is assumed to be above politics as a matter of unanimous convention. And unlike England, the intellectual center here is filled not by European imports (although they play a considerable role) but by an unquestioned ethic of objectivity and realism, based essentially on an epistemology of separation and difference. Thus each field is separate from the others because the subject matter is separate. Each separation corresponds immediately to a separation in function, institution, history and purpose. Each discourse "represents" the field, which in turn is supported by its own constituency and the specialized audience to which it appeals. The mark of true professionalism is accuracy of representation of society, vindicated in the case of sociology, for instance, by a direct correlation between representation of society and corporate and/or governmental interests, a role in social policy-making, access to political authority. Literary studies, conversely, are realistically *not* about society but about masterpieces in need of periodic adulation and appreciation. Such correlations make possible the use of words like "objectivity," "realism" and "moderation" when used in sociology or in literary criticism. And these notions in turn assure their own confirmation by careful selectivity of evidence, the incorporation and subsequent neutralization of dissent (also known as pluralism) and networks of insiders, experts whose presence is due to their conformity, not to any rigorous judgment of their past performance (the good team player always turns up).

But I must press on, even though there are numerous qualifications and refinements to be added at this point (e.g., the organized relationship between clearly affiliated fields such as political science and sociology versus the use by one field of another unrelated one for the purposes of national policy issues; the network of patronage and the insider/outsider dichotomy; the strange cultural encouragement of theories stressing such "components" of the structure of power as chance, morality, American innocence, decentralized egos, etc.). The particular mission of the humanities is, in the aggregate, to represent *noninterference* in the affairs of the everyday world. As we have seen, there has been a historical erosion in the role of letters since the New Criticism, and I have suggested that the conjuncture of a narrowly based university environment for technical language and literature studies with the self-policing, self-purifying communities erected even by Marxist, as well as other disciplinary, discourses, produced a very small but definite function for the humanities: to represent humane marginality, which is also to preserve and if possible to conceal the hierarchy of powers that occupy the center, define the social terrain, and fix the limits of use functions, fields, marginality and so on. Some of the corollaries of this role for the humanities generally and literary criticism in particular are that the institutional presence of humanities guarantees a space for the deployment of free-floating abstractions (scholarship, taste, tact, humanism) that are defined in advance as indefinable; that when it is not easily domesticated, "theory" is employable as a discourse of occultation and legitimation; that self-regulation is the ethos behind which the institutional humanities allow and in a sense encourage the unrestrained operation of market forces that were traditionally thought of as subject to ethical and philosophical review.

Very broadly stated, then, noninterference for the humanist means laissez-faire: "they" can run the country, we will explicate Wordsworth and Schlegel. It does not stretch things greatly to note that noninterference and rigid specialization in the academy are directly related to what has been called a counterattack by "highly mobilized business elites" in reaction to the immediately preceding period during which national needs were thought of as fulfilled by resources allocated collectively and democratically. However, working through foundations, think tanks, sectors of the academy, and the government, corporate elites according to David Dickson and David Noble "proclaimed a new age of reason while remystifying reality." This involved a set of "interrelated" epistemological and ideological imperatives, which are an extrapolation from the noninterference I spoke about earlier. Each of these imperatives is in congruence with the way intellectual and academic "fields" view themselves internally and across the dividing lines:

1. The rediscovery of the self-regulating market, the wonders of free enterprise, and the classical liberal attack on government regulation of the economy, all in the name of liberty.
2. The reinvention of the idea of progress, now cast in terms of "innovation" and "reindustrialization," and the limitation of expectations and social welfare in the quest for productivity.
3. The attack on democracy, in the name of "efficiency," "manageability," "governability," "rationality," and "competence."
4. The remystification of science through the promotion of formalized decision methodologies, the restoration of the authority of expertise, and the renewed use of science as legitimation for social policy through deepening industry ties to universities and other "free" institutions of policy analysis and recommendation.[11]

In other words, (1) says that literary criticism minds its own business and is "free" to do what it wishes with no community responsibility whatever. Hence at one end of the scale, for instance, is the recent successful attack on the NEH for funding too many socially determined programs and, at the other end, the proliferation of private critical languages with an absurdist bent presided over paradoxically by "big name professors," who also extoll the virtues of humanism, pluralism and humane scholarship. Retranslated, (2) has meant that the number of jobs for young graduates has shrunk dramatically as the "inevitable" result of market forces, which in turn prove the marginality of scholarship that is premised on its own harmless social obsolescence. This has created a demand for sheer innovation and indiscriminate publication (e.g., the sudden increase in advanced critical journals; the departmental need for experts and courses in theory and structuralism), and it has virtually destroyed the career trajectory and social horizons of young people within the system. Imperatives (3) and (4) have meant the recrudescence of strict professionalism for sale to any client, deliberately oblivious of the complicity between the academy, the government and the corporations, decorously silent on the large questions of social, economic and foreign policy.

Very well: if what I have been saying has any validity, then the politics of interpretation demand a dialectical response from a critical consciousness worthy of its name. Instead of noninterference and specialization, there must be *interference*, crossing of borders and obstacles, a determined attempt to generalize exactly at those points where generalizations seem impossible to make. One of the first interferences to be ventured, then, is a crossing from literature, which is supposed to be subjective and powerless, into those exactly parallel realms, now covered by journalism and the production of information, that employ representation but are supposed to be objective and powerful. Here we have a superb guide in John Berger, in whose most recent work there is the basis of a major critique of modern representation. Berger suggests that if we regard photography as coeval in its origins with sociology and positivism (and I would add the classic realistic novel), we see that

> what they shared was the hope that observable quantifiable facts, recorded by experts, would constitute the proven truth that humanity required. Precision would replace metaphysics; planning would resolve conflicts. What happened, instead, was that the way was opened to a view of the world in which everything and everybody could be reduced to a factor in a calculation, and the calculation was profit.[12]

Much of the world today is represented in this way: as the McBride Commission Report has it, a tiny handful of large and powerful oligarchies control about ninety percent of the world's information and communication flows. This domain, staffed by experts and media executives, is, as Herbert Schiller and others have shown, affiliated to an even smaller number of governments, at the very same time that the rhetoric of objectivity, balance, realism and freedom covers what is being done. And for the most part, such consumer items as "the news"—a euphemism for ideological images of the world that determine political reality for a vast majority of the world's population—hold forth, untouched by interfering secular and critical minds, who for all sorts of obvious reasons are not hooked into the systems of power.

This is not the place, nor is there time, to advance a fully articulated program of interference. I can only suggest in conclusion that we need to think about breaking out of the disciplinary ghettos in which as intellectuals we have been confined, to reopen the blocked social processes ceding objective representation (hence power) of the world to a small coterie of experts and their clients, to consider that the audience for literacy is not a closed circle of three thousand professional critics but the community of human beings living in society, and to regard social reality in a secular rather than a mystical mode, despite all the protestations about realism and objectivity.

Two concrete tasks—again adumbrated by Berger—strike me as particularly useful. One is to use the visual faculty (which also happens to be dominated by visual media such as television, news photography and commercial film, all of them fundamentally immediate, "objective" and ahistorical) to restore the nonsequential energy of lived historical memory and subjectivity as fundamental components of meaning in representation. Berger calls this an alternative use of photography: using photomontage to tell other stories than the official sequential or ideological ones produced by institutions of power. (Superb examples are Sarah Graham-Brown's photo-essay *The Palestinians and Their Society* and Susan Meisalas's *Nicaragua*.) Second is opening the culture to experiences of the Other which have remained "outside" (and have been repressed or framed in a context of confrontational hostility) the norms manufactured by "insiders." An excellent example is Malek Alloula's *Le Harem colonial,* a study of early twentieth-century postcards and photographs of Algerian harem women. The pictorial capture of colonized people by colonizer, which signifies power, is reenacted by a young Algerian sociologist, Alloula, who sees his own fragmented history in the pictures, then reinscribes this history in his text as the result of understanding and making that intimate experience intelligible for an audience of modern European readers.

In both instances, finally, we have the recovery of a history hitherto either misrepresented or rendered invisible. Stereotypes of the Other have always been connected to political actualities of one sort or another, just as the truth of lived communal (or personal) experience has often been totally sublimated in official narratives, institutions and ideologies. But in having attempted—and perhaps even successfully accomplishing—this recovery, there is the crucial next phase: connecting these more politically vigilant forms of interpretation to an ongoing political and social praxis. Short of making that connection, even the best-intentioned and the cleverest interpretive activity is bound to sink back into the murmur of mere prose. For to move from interpretation to its politics is in large measure to go from undoing to doing, and this, given the currently accepted divisions between criticism and art, is risking all the discomfort of a great unsettlement in ways of seeing and doing. One must refuse to believe, however, that the comforts of specialized habits can be so seductive as to keep us all in our assigned places.

References

1. See Ronald Steel, *Walter Lippmann and the American Century* (Boston: Little, Brown & Co., 1980), pp. 180-85 and 212-16.
2. Antonio Gramsci to Tatiana Schucht, in Giuseppe Fiori, *Antonio Gramsci: Life of a Revolutionary,* trans. Tom Nairn (London: Dutton, 1970), p. 74.
3. Gramsci to Schucht, *Lettere dal Carcere* (Turin: G. Einauci, 1975), p. 466; my translation.
4. Gramsci, *Selections from the Prison Notebooks,* trans. Quintin Hoare and Geoffrey Nowell Smith (New York: International Publishers, 1971), p. 171.
5. Fredric Jameson, *The Political Unconscious* (Ithaca: Cornell University Press, 1981), p. 10: all further references to this work will be included in the text. Perhaps not incidentally, what Jameson claims for Marxism here is made the central feature of 19th-century British fiction by Deirdre David, *Fictions of Resolutions in Three Victorian Novels* (New York: Columbia University Press, 1980).
6. Terry Eagleton, "The Idealism of American Criticism," *New Left Review* 127 (May-June 1981): 59.
7. J. Hillis Miller, "The Function of Rhetorical Study at the Present Time," *ADE Bulletin* (September 1979): 12.
8. Robert Darnton, "A Journeyman's Life under the Old Regime: Work and Culture in an Eighteenth-Century Printing Shop," Princeton Alumni Weekly, 7 (September 1981): 12.
9. Michael Bakunin, *Selected Writings,* ed. and trans. Arthur Lehning (London: Cape, 1973), p. 160.
10. See Perry Anderson, "Components of the National Culture," in *Student Power,* ed. Alexander Cockburn and Robin Blackburn (London: Harmondsworth, Penguin; NLR, 1969).
11. David Dickson and David Noble, "By Force of Reason: The Politics of Science and Policy," in *The Hidden Election,* ed. Thomas Ferguson and Joel Rogers (New York: Pantheon, 1981), p. 267.
12. John Berger, "Another Way of Telling," *Journal of Social Reconstruction* 1 (January-March 1980): 64.